UNIVERSITY OF WASHINGTON PUBLICATIONS
IN LANGUAGE AND LITERATURE, VOLUME 14

PROWESS AND CHARITY

IN THE PERCEVAL OF CHRÉTIEN DE TROYES

BY DAVID C. FOWLER

University of Washington Press   Seattle

This book is published with assistance
from a grant by the Ford Foundation.

© *1959 by the University of Washington Press*
Library of Congress Catalog Card Number: 59-9703
Lithographed in the United States of America

For
Mary Gene
Sandra
Caroline

CONTENTS

Contents

PROWESS AND CHARITY

IN THE PERCEVAL OF CHRÉTIEN DE TROYES

INTRODUCTION

My purpose in the following pages is to examine the *Perceval* or *Conte del Graal* of the twelfth-century poet, Chrétien de Troyes, and to elucidate what I consider to be the meaning of the poem as Chrétien intended it. My conclusion, briefly stated, is that the poet has constructed his narrative so as to reveal the "internal quest" of the hero, Perceval, for the resolution of a conflict of ideals within himself. The ideals in conflict are prowess *(proesce)* and charity, or the love of God *(charité)*. Taken together, these concepts were the cornerstone of chivalry in the twelfth century. That these two ideals were inimical and that charity must ultimately prevail over prowess together constitute Chrétien's theme. It follows from this that the poem does not merely reflect the aristocratic ideals of the age, but rather that it challenges the very foundation of feudal society. Finally, the profundity of the poem's theme and the skill with which this theme is made evident throughout the text (insofar as its incompleteness allows) lead me to suggest that the *Perceval* should rank first among the romances of Chrétien; that it is, indeed, a great poem; and that its horizon extends far beyond the century of its birth.

Before we begin our examination of the text it will be necessary, first, to determine what factors have tended in the past to obscure the meaning of the poem, and, second, to make clear the relation of our proposed interpretation to medieval poetic theory. The relevance of these topics to the subsequent

3

analysis will, I trust, be a sufficient excuse for the digression
that follows.

One factor that has retarded the study of the poem in its own
terms has been the grail itself. Since the text of the *Perceval*
contains the earliest account of this fascinating talisman, a
tremendous amount of *Perceval* scholarship has naturally ac-
cumulated, but most of these studies, though not all, [1] have
focused on the grail *per se,* with the result that the poem as
a whole has been obscured--to borrow Chrétien's figure--like
the stars at sunrise. This grail scholarship, together with related source studies, is of course extremely valuable, as I
hope to show, in any close reading of the poem. All that needs
to be stressed here is that the interpretation proposed in the
following pages expresses what I take to be the meaning, not
of the poet's source or sources, but of the poem as Chrétien
composed it.

A second factor tending to obscure the meaning of the poem--
related to the first--is the subtle influence of the *Perceval*
continuations, written after Chrétien's death, which in some
cases contain developments of motifs suggested in Chrétien's
text. One example will suffice. In the *Perceval,* the hero's
cousin tells him of a smith, Trebuchet, the only person who
can mend his sword (3673 ff.). Now since the *Perceval* is un-
finished, and since in the continuations Trebuchet actually appears, there has been a fairly widespread (though not universal) assumption that this smith had a role later on in the
source, beyond the point where Chrétien stopped, and that the
continuators were simply completing the narrative. This hy-
pothesis has obscured the fact, as we shall see, that the smith
is actually Chrétien's hermit, and that the whole passage dealing with Trebuchet is part of an elaborate preparation for the
climactic scene at the hermitage on Good Friday. It is significant, I think, that Loomis, in his reconstruction of the vengeance theme, considers the smith an intrusion. [2]

There is, finally, one feature of the poem itself that has
stood in the way of interpreters, and that is the family relationships mentioned to Perceval by the hermit in the Good
Friday episode. The holy man tells Perceval that the king who
is served with the grail is his (the hermit's) brother, that Perceval's mother is their sister, and that the fisher king, he

believes, is the son of the king who is served with the grail. It should be recognized, I think, that this genealogy is not intended to be realistic. Near the beginning of the poem Perceval's mother tells him about the deaths of his father and his two brothers, and says that he, Perceval, was all she had left in the way of a family (484-88): '"You were all my comfort and all my wealth; for there were no more of my people *(Car il n'i avoit plus des miens):* nothing more had God left me of which I was joyous and glad.'"[3] Hence to take the hermit's statement as realistic is to assume an ignorance of her own family on the part of Perceval's mother, which has no visible function in the poem. And the presumption, on the other hand, that Chrétien here has simply slipped up, though it provides an easy escape, does not, I submit, show sufficient respect for his craftsmanship.

Then what is the function of the hermit's genealogy? It is in one sense a "recognition" device of the sort which Chrétien uses elsewhere in his romances,[4] and which in fact became very popular in later Arthurian tradition. Readers of the *Morte d'Arthur* will recall that at the end of the most somber otherworld journeys Malory turns up the houselights, so to speak, and the major participants in the adventure recognize and greet each other in the unmistakable atmosphere of this world. This phenomenon is particularly evident in *Sir Gareth of Orkeney* and in the conversation between Bors and Lancelot added by Malory at the end of his *Sankgreal.*[5] In the *Perceval,* however, the genealogy is much more than a mere device, and the recognition that results from it is far deeper than is the case in any of Chrétien's other poems. For the present I shall content myself with pointing out that the family relationships mentioned by the hermit serve to tighten the circle of the hero's experiences and to help provide the final resolution of his internal quest. More will be said later.

Before we come to a direct analysis of the poem there now remains only the necessity of making clear what is intended when we speak of the "meaning" of a romance such as Chrétien's and of indicating the relationship between the interpretation offered in this study and medieval poetics in general.

By "meaning" I refer specifically to the *sententia,* or core of truth, which, in the medieval view, should be at the heart

of all serious poetry regardless of the nature of its exterior,
or surface, meaning. Undoubtedly the most articulate scholar
dealing with this area of study in recent years is D. W. Robertson, Jr.[6] Briefly, Roberston explains that medieval poetic
doctrine sprang ultimately from the concept of scriptural exegesis developed in the Middle Ages, in which a distinction,
suggested by St. Paul's statement (II Cor. 3:6), was made between the "letter" and the "spirit. " Beginning with a passage
from Alanus de Insulis, *De planctu naturae,* he calls attention
to the terminology used by Nature to define poetry, e. g., *cortex,* referring to the "letter" or historical sense, and *nucleus,*
referring to the higher meaning or "spirit" of poetry. Other
terms are *pictura,* designating the artificial combination of
elements which provides the surface of the poem, and *con-
junctura,* the construction of a *cortex,* or poetic surface, in
such a way as to reveal the *nucleus,* or inner meaning of the
poem. He goes on to say specifically (citing Hugh of St. Victor) that in the twelfth century there developed a somewhat
specialized, tripartite terminology that distinguished the *lit-
tera* (essentially a study of the language of a text), the *sensus*
(surface or historical meaning--the "letter" according to the
more traditional terminology), and the *sententia* (the *nucleus,*
that is, the higher meaning or "spirit" of a poem). He then
shows, I believe, that Chrétien knew these terms and used
them. Robertson concludes by pointing out that poetry in the
Middle Ages was considered an adjunct of charity, the fundamental law of Christian love which was the basis of all medieval theology, and that all serious Christian poetry can be ex-
pected to conduce to charity on the level of *sententia:* "It was
the function of the medieval poet to keep this great civilizing
concept [charity] alive and active for his own special audience,
to prevent that audience from becoming a multitude of those
who have ears and hear not. "[7] With this brief summary of Robertson's presentation before us, then, we may now state, in
the language of twelfth-century poetic doctrine, that the *sententia* of Chrétien's *Perceval* is the triumph of charity over
prowess.
    To what Robertson has to say about medieval literary ter-
minology I now wish to add a few observations relating more
specifically to the actual process of composition, since this

was not his primary concern in the article summarized above. First, it is important to realize the polemical cast of the statements used by Robertson in his formulation of medieval poetic doctrine. Throughout most of the Middle Ages, and certainly in the twelfth century, Christian humanists like Alanus de Insulis were arrayed against those who denounced the study of pagan literature.[8] Hence most of their statements arise as answers to hostile charges and usually constitute justifications of the study of the classics, a defense of poetry as it were, rather than direct statements about poetic composition. Nature's definition of poetry in Alanus de Insulis, *De planctu naturae,* which Robertson cites, is in response to the poet's purposely naïve question about the escapades of Jupiter, Bacchus, and Apollo in classical literature. It is hazardous, therefore, to regard statements growing out of a defense of poetry as inevitably equivalent to a theory of composition, even when the poets themselves (like Chrétien) use the terminology, since it is clearly to the poet's advantage to utilize whatever he can find in the way of theory for the defense of his craft. That Chrétien regarded poetry as an adjunct of charity is, I believe, entirely true, as will be seen in my interpretation of his *Perceval;* but that his *sententia* is in any way constructed on the analogy of scriptural exegesis seems to me an altogether unlikely assumption.[9]

More important for an understanding of Chrétien's poetic art is the fact, clearly established by Muscatine and others, that the twelfth century saw a marked development in the "capacity of the age to deal with the inner life and to see the mechanism of the soul in sharp definition."[10] Muscatine derives his evidence for this statement, not from any twelfth-century psychological theory (there was none as such), but from the actual poetic practices revealed in a large number of romances of the period. His concern, however, is largely the *Liebesmonolog,* or internal debate, in its relation to the development of psychological allegory. And it is interesting to note that he finds Chrétien somewhat given to preciosity in his use of the device, while the best examples are to be found in what everyone would agree, I am sure, are inferior romances when compared with Chretien's. 1 shall not consider this problem here in any detail, but I suggest that Chrétien's relative in-

difference to the *Liebesmonolog* can be explained by the fact
that his psychological method goes far beyond the limits of this
rather mechanical device: specifically, I believe that his delineation of the "inner life," the "mechanism of the soul," is
to be found in his projection of characterization in the narrative structure. It is in this sense that Chrétien's *Perceval*
sets forth the "internal quest" of the hero.

Finally, before we turn to an analysis of the *Perceval,* we
need to consider briefly the relation of Chrétien as a poet to
his sources. That these sources included an impressive array
of myth, primarily Celtic, appears to be well established. But
how did Chrétien regard his sources? A common (though by no
means universal) assumption seems to be that he saw them
simply as *matière,* that is, a collection of miscellaneous characters and narratives which he could maneuver in various ways
in order to produce an attractive and courtly design. Certain-
ly--so goes the theory--he did not "understand" them. This
supposition seems to me unlikely in the extreme, and contrary
to all we know of the relation between poets and their sources.
It is all the more dubious to attribute such insensitivity to a
poet of Chrétien's psychological acuity. Rather, as I hope to
show, Chrétien responded profoundly to the suggestiveness of
his sources, and, through the agency of what Cicero *(De ora-
tore* ii. 46) called the poetic *furor,* by means of which a poem
is distinguished from a metrical treatise, he created a beautiful conjunction of "letter" and "spirit."

To conclude this rather extended but necessary preamble,
I should like to quote from W. A. Nitze's recent study, *Perceval and the Holy Grail:*

> It is pertinent then to repeat a truism. The proper approach to
> the *Perceval* is the *Perceval.* It should first of all be read for its
> own sake, for what it means as a story and as the expression of the
> poet's ideas and art. Then it should be considered with reference
> to its sources, the background of material which went into its com-
> position. Chrétien was a medieval man, trained in the clerical meth-
> od of exegesis or exposition. His meaning is often imposed on his
> material, though it is also inspired by it; the two processes are
> linked. But for the reader of his romance, the meaning comes
> first. [11]

Nitze ends his essay with the following statement: "Chrétien de Troyes not only made the novel or *roman* in France an independent composition, he centered its interest on psychology. Of this the *Perceval* is an outstanding example. It fascinated the poet's contemporaries, and it is worthy of our admiration today."

I. THE FOREST OF WALES
(69-634)

The hero, Perceval (not mentioned by name until after the grail episode), is brought up by his mother in a waste forest and knows nothing of knighthood. One day by chance riding in the forest he encounters five knights and is fascinated by their appearance. Returning home he tells his mother that he is going forth to become a knight. Grief-stricken, his mother tells him that his father was a knight but had been wounded in the legs, crippled, and later died of grief over the slaying of two of his sons, who had just been knighted. Perceval, she says, was little more than two when they retired to the forest to live, and she had hoped to bring him up in ignorance of knighthood. Seeing that he is determined to go, however, she gives him instructions in how to behave in the presence of ladies and noble men, and especially, she tells him, be sure to pray in church. "Mother," says Perceval, "what is church?" She then tells him of the sufferings of Jesus Christ, and he promises her that he will do as she says. After he has ridden a short distance, he looks back and sees that his mother has fallen down in a faint as if she were dead, whereupon he strikes his mount with a switch and rides off into the forest.

In the short space of 565 lines, Chrétien presents a series of brilliant scenes from which we emerge with a clear picture of the untutored but promising hero, his family history, his mother's concern, and, finally, his determination to become a knight. It is not an exaggeration to say that the foundation for every single episode to follow in the romance is laid in this

10

section. The narrative flows, however, as effortlessly as if the poet were thinking of nothing but the scene he is presently describing, and the range of his effects extends from high comedy to high seriousness. Perceval's encounter with the knights is pure hilarity, while his mother's account of his father and two brothers is serious, even somber.

Yet, despite the complexity of purpose and the range of effects evident in this section, Chrétien's main theme, the conflict of prowess and charity, emerges clearly and dramatically. The very first words of Perceval, when he hears the sound of ringing armor in the forest, reveal his instinctive reliance on prowess as a basis for action. He thinks the noise of the armor he hears must be coming from devils (113-24):

"By my soul, my mother, my lady, told me true, who told me that devils are more noisy than anything in the world. And she said, to teach me, that because of them ought one to cross himself. But this instruction shall I disdain, for never indeed will I cross myself, rather will I strike the strongest so quickly with one of my javelins that never, as I believe, will any of the others approach me."

But when the knights actually appear, of course, he is so impressed by the sight of them that he concludes they are angels, and their leader is God Himself (150-58): "'My mother herself said that one is to believe and adore God and bow to him and honor him, so I shall adore this one and all the others with him.' Straightway he throws himself to the ground and says all the creed and prayers that he knew, which his mother had taught him." The idea here expressed of prowess worshiped by Perceval as if it were the God his mother taught him to love is treated with amused irony. Later on, however, as we shall see, this inversion of values will emerge as the fundamental crisis in Perceval's quest for self-realization.

In the passages just discussed we can observe that Perceval's mother tried to inculcate the love of God in her son. Through her references to his father, on the other hand, we learn that the latter was of great reputation as a knight (416-19): "'There was no knight of such great worth, so dreaded nor so feared, fair son, as your father was in all the Isles of the Sea.'" She goes on to tell him that his father advised his two sons (Perceval's older brothers) to become knights, and de-

scribes how they were overcome in combat and so died. Thus
Chrétien establishes, with great psychological penetration, the
conflict of ideals in the hero's parents. His father represents
prowess, his mother charity. But the opposition is not as
simple as I have stated it. Perceval's mother, in telling him
how his father was wounded and became a cripple, reflects
bitterly on the fact that the good must fall *(les bons decheoir
estuet)* (428-34): "'. . . it is well known in many places that
misfortunes happen to the worthy men who maintain themselves
in great honor and in prowess. Baseness, shame nor laziness
does not fall, for it cannot; but the good must fall.'" Perhaps
in the account of the suffering of his father she intends to turn
Perceval from his desire for knighthood: prowess inevitably
leads to this--so runs her argument. Yet at the same time her
statement that *les bons decheoir estuet,* applied bitterly to the
past, may likewise refer to her son's future, though in a different sense: Perceval must "fall" before he can achieve self-
realization. She cannot keep him forever hidden in the forest
of Wales.

II. THE MAIDEN OF THE TENT
(635-833)

The next morning Perceval rides until he comes to a beautifully adorned tent in a meadow. Mistaking it for a church he goes inside, where he finds a damsel asleep on a bed. Following his mother's advice about behavior in the presence of ladies (so he thinks), he greets her, kisses her roughly, and then forcibly takes a ring from her finger. While she pleads with him in tears, he sits down to eat at a table spread with fine food and drink. Then abruptly he departs, commending her to God. Soon the maiden's *ami* returns and, suspecting that she has been false, swears that he will never stop until he has taken the Welshman's head. And she must follow him, on foot and in rags if necessary, until this justice is accomplished.

This scene is the first projection of the counsel of the hero's mother and stands in contrast to Perceval's relative sophistication in the Belrepeire episode (V, below). But, like virtually every scene in Chrétien's poem, it has a multiple function. Here we find set in motion a series of events which will lead to the death of the *ami* of Perceval's cousin (episode VII, below), and the shameful condition of the wretched maiden (episode VIII): both will be the evil consequences of the hero's ignorant actions. Most important, however, is the fact that in this scene Perceval mistakes the tent for a church, and vows to go in and pray to God for something to eat (655-66):

"God! now I see your house. I should make a mistake if I did not

13

go to adore you. Indeed my mother told me the truth when she told
me that a minster was the most beautiful thing there is, and she
told me that I should never find a church that I should not go in it
to adore the Creator, in whom I believe. I shall go pray him, by
my faith, that He give me today to eat, for I have great need of it. "

It is impossible to overlook the irony of these remarks: the difference between Perceval's and his mother's understanding of
what constitutes the "beauty" of the house of God; the worldly,
courtly setting in which he finds the maiden whom he unknow-
ingly vows to adore; and above all, I think, the fact that he intends to pray to God for food. He does find food, of course,
but he is destined not to learn the kind of "food" that God provides (i.e., the Host) until he reaches the lowly hermitage on
Good Friday (episode XII). It is interesting to note, however,
looking ahead for a moment, that at Belrepeire (episode V)
Perceval actually finds two minsters, but they are in poor condition, not beautiful, and, like the castle itself, are destitute
of food (1756-70):

There were two minsters in the town which were two abbeys, the
one of trembling nuns, the other of dejected monks. He did not find
the minsters well adorned nor well tapestried, rather he saw the
walls cracked and split and the towers uncovered and the houses
were open night and day. No mill grinds there, nor oven bakes in
any place in the whole castle, nor was there bread nor cake nor anything which might be sold by which one might gain a denier.

But the hero's only apparent response to this--noble in its way
--is to agree to do something about it, that is, to free the town
and its inhabitants from the siege by the exercise of his prowess. Thus when he comes to the grail castle, as we shall see,
he is not yet able to recognize the Host in the grail, to ask who
is served with it, or, in short, to understand its significance
at all. Not until he finds the hermit will he be able to com-
prehend the divine imperative (John 6:27): "Labour not for the
meat which perisheth, but for the meat which endureth unto
everlasting life. "

III. THE COURT OF ARTHUR
(834-1304)

Meanwhile Perceval is directed to the court of Arthur, who will make him a knight. On his way there he meets a knight armed all in red, carrying a cup of gold which he has taken from the king. Perceval rides on into the court, where the king, still distracted by the theft of the cup, does not notice him. Finally aroused from his meditation, Arthur agrees to make him knight. Perceval then asks the king for the arms of the red knight whom he had seen earlier. "Go take them, they are yours," says Keu the seneschal in his customary sardonic manner. In the hall is a maiden who had not smiled for over six years, of whom the court fool had prophesied that she would not smile until she saw the best of knights. As Perceval is about to leave, this maiden smiles at him and says she believes he will be the best knight in the world. Keu, angered by this, strikes her to the ground and kicks the fool into the fire. Perceval rides out to where the red knight is waiting, and, wasting no time, pierces him through the eye with his javelin so that he falls dead to the ground. Putting on the red armor, he sends a young squire back to the court with the cup for Arthur, and with a message to the maiden whom Keu struck, promising to avenge her that blow.

The primary function of this episode is to begin the process of "civilizing" the hero. He becomes a knight; he kills his first antagonist. To be sure, Perceval's uncouthness is still the subject of much comedy, but the fact that he possesses a certain inner quality clearly emerges in Chrétien's account (972-78):

"'Make me a knight, lord king,' says he, 'for I wish to go away.' Clear and laughing were the eyes in the head of the wild youth. No one who sees him considers him wise, but all those who saw him held him for handsome and gentle."

Comedy is again evident in what happens following the death of the red knight. Perceval pulls and tugs at the knight's armor but cannot get it free of his body. The young squire, Yonez, who has been watching him, is amused at this and comes over to help him. But, when he suggests that Perceval remove the Welsh clothes his mother had provided for him and put on the fine garments of the dead knight, Perceval refuses (1161-64): "'The devil! is this now a joke that I should change my good clothes, that my mother made for me the other day, for the clothes of this knight?'"

The hero has completed the first phase of his education for knighthood. But in the retention of his old clothes we see him still consciously respecting his mother's influence. It will be the task of his tutor, Gornemant de Goort, to remove the last vestiges of this conscious reliance on his mother. Ironically, however, it is precisely at this point, as we shall see, when every outward trace of maternal influence (in dress and speech) has been eradicated, that Perceval experiences the first pangs of conscience over his cruel abandonment of his mother. As Chrétien remarks (1173): "It's a very heavy thing to teach a fool. . . ." *(Mout griés chose est de fol aprandre.)*

IV. GORNEMANT DE GOORT

(1305-1698)

Perceval rides until he comes to a stately castle beside the sea. The lord of the castle, Gornemant de Goort, greets him very courteously and, inviting him in, teaches him the use of arms and instructs him in the manners and customs of the noble life. Gornemant is quite taken by the youth, who is an apt pupil, and he invites him to stay a year if he so desires. But Perceval now for the first time thinks of how he left his mother grief-stricken and tells his tutor that he is determined to leave the following dawn.

This episode constitutes the second projection of the advice of the hero's mother: seek the company and counsel of worthy men *(prodomes)*. Gornemant de Goort is of course assuming the role that would have been played by Perceval's father, had he been alive. Chrétien perhaps gives us a hint of this in describing (1352-59) Perceval's first glimpse of the noble man, standing on the drawbridge, accompanied by two youths, and holding a small staff for support. The *bastonet* which he was holding *par contenance* may simply be a walking stick--for Gornemant was not a cripple--yet it seems highly reminiscent of the crippled condition of Perceval's father. This one hint, however, is all we have. The main purpose of the whole interlude is to give the hero his chivalric education, and, as we have already seen, to strip him of the surviving traces of his mother's influence, represented by the crude Welsh clothes and his habit of talking interminably about what his mother taught him.

17

When it is apparent to the noble man that Perceval is determined to go in search of his mother, he goes to the youth early
the next morning and presents him with a complete set of new
clothes (1607-13): '"Friend, you will put on these clothes that
you see here, if you believe me.' The youth answers: 'Fair
lord, you could say much better; the clothes that my mother
made me then are they not worth more than these, and you
wish that I put these on?'" In response to these objections the
lord reminds him of his promise to heed his commands, and
so Perceval obeys (1622-23): "He does not delay any longer in
putting on the clothes, so has he left those his mother gave
him."

Next his tutor puts on his spurs (as the one who knights him
should do) and gives him advice on how to conduct himself--ad-
vice that, as was the case with the new clothes, is designed to
replace the counsel of his mother. Gornemant teaches him to
heed an opponent's request for mercy, warns him against too
much talking, instructs him to counsel ladies in distress, and,
finally, urges him to go to church and pray the Creator for
mercy and for protection "in this earthly world" (an cest siegle
terriien, 1669). Perceval is stirred by this reminiscence of
his mother's advice (1672-74): '"By all the apostles of Rome
may you be blessed, fair lord, for I heard my mother say the
same.'"

But his teacher warns him against speaking of his mother
(1675-84):

"Now don't ever again say, fair brother," says the worthy man,
"that your mother taught and instructed you. I do not blame you if
you have said it up to now, but from now on, by your mercy, I pray
you that you take heed. If you said it any more people would hold it
for folly, for this I pray you beware of it."

Perceval is now recreated in the image of his tutor, Gornemant de Goort, who stands for everything that is best in the
high order of knighthood. He is a skilled instructor, both in
the tools of prowess and in the chivalric code of behavior which
owes its grace to a professed devotion to charity, the love of
God. But, when Perceval naïvely equates the advice to attend
church with his mother's counsel, Gornemant reacts sharply,
commanding him to stop talking about his mother. In this reac-

tion Gornemant reveals the fact that indeed the two are not the
same: the ultimate purpose of piety in the knight is to obtain
protection "in this earthly world," however attractive and per-
suasive may be the ideological shield with which he hides this
fact from himself and from others. True charity must yield to
the sovereignty of prowess in the chivalric code. But Perceval
has yet to learn that, as it is written, *no man can serve two
masters.*

V. BELREPEIRE

(1699-2973)

Having bidden farewell to his tutor, the hero now rides off in search of his mother. Soon he comes to a castle in a wasteland, where he is humbly but hospitably received by Blancheflor, the beautiful lady of the castle. That night she comes to his bedside weeping, and tells him that the castle is besieged by the forces of her enemy, Clamadeu, to whom she is on the point of yielding. Perceval hints that he will be able to help her, and they spend the night together, lying arm in arm and mouth to mouth. The following day he defeats Anguingueron, the seneschal, but shows mercy and sends him to Arthur's court. Clamadeu learns of the defeat of his seneschal and tightens the siege in order to force capitulation, but a barge loaded with food reaches Belrepeire, and the inhabitants are saved from starvation. Clamadeu then challenges Perceval to single combat and is defeated. Again the hero shows mercy and directs his victim to Arthur. The two men report to King Arthur, who is grieved that Perceval himself is not there. Meanwhile the hero takes leave of his dear friend Blancheflor, though she is reluctant to see him go, and promises to return after he has found his mother.

This episode presents the instructions of Gornemant de Goort translated into action. Although the hero's naïve conformity to his tutor's advice is amusingly described, the pure comedy of the earlier scenes is gone. Perceval has now achieved a degree of poise. If he is silent in the company of Blancheflor, it is not because he is overawed by her beauty, but be-

cause he remembers the noble man's warning against too much
talking. When she finally breaks the silence, he learns that
she is his tutor's niece--which is Chrétien's way of saying
that she is an "adjunct" of chivalry. She will provide the hero with an opportunity to put into practice the second command: the counseling of ladies. In describing how relaxed and
comfortable Perceval was in bed that night, Chrétien stresses
his complete innocence of the delights of women (1935-44):

> The knight had that night all the ease and all the delight that one
> might know how to devise in a bed, except only the delight of maiden,
> if it might please him, or of lady, if it were allowed him. But he
> knew nothing of that, nor did he think of it either little or much, and
> he soon went to sleep, for he was not worried about anything.

It is therefore futile, I think, to argue the question of Perceval's relations with Blancheflor, for to do so is to miss the
enjoyment which Chrétien intended in his amusing tableau:
perfect innocence sleeping all night arm in arm--and mouth
to mouth--with seduction. Or, from another point of view,
the hero poised on the threshold of experience. I do not believe that Chrétien wished to take him beyond this point because, as I hope to show, the significant realm of Perceval's
experience does not lie in this direction, and an excursion into
the sphere of Lancelot would have disturbed the delicate bal-
ancing of opposites which is so brilliant a feature of this scene.
   The granting of mercy to an opponent is of course illustrated in the hero's defeat of the seneschal and Clamadeu, both of
whom he sends to Arthur. But there is an important point here
that should not be overlooked. In both cases his opponent pleads
with him not to be handed over either to Blancheflor or to Gornemant de Goort. When Perceval orders Anguingueron to report to Blancheflor, the seneschal says (2276-83): "'Then slay
me, for she too would have me slain, for she desires nothing
so much as my death and my sorrow because I had a hand in
the death of her father, and I have done her so much harm that
I have this year taken from her all her knights, either dead or
captured.'" And similarly of the noble Gornemant he says
(2304-12):

> "There I do not know my protection," says he, "fair lord, where
> you send me; so help me God, in evil ways and in evil hands do you

wish to place me, for in this war I slew for him one of his brothers german. Slay me, fair sweet friend, rather than make me go to him; there will be my death, if you drive me there."

For fear that vengeance might be taken on his victims, therefore, Perceval orders them to report to Arthur. In doing this he shows his superiority to both his tutor and his lady, even though, of course, he himself is not directly involved in the feud. Particularly sharp is the contrast between the external system of conduct, which calls for the subordination of mercy to blood revenge (an aspect of charity subordinated to an aspect of prowess), and the wellspring of mercy revealed in Perceval. It is clear that this mercy in the hero is spontaneous, not inculcated; for he was not taught what to do should mercy be requested by the slayer of his tutor's brother, or by the man responsible for the death of his lady's father. We have here not simply the case of the student surpassing the master, but rather the first clear revelation of an inner quality of the hero that is to take him far beyond the mere acquisition of a knightly reputation. The prophecy of the smiling maiden in Arthur's court now begins to look like something more than hyperbole.

VI. THE GRAIL CASTLE
(2974-3421)

Perceval takes his leave of the grieving monks and nuns of Belrepeire, having promised to return to them with his mother, or else, if she has died, to make generous provision for annual services for her soul. He rides all day fully armed without meeting anyone to show him the way until he comes to a river, where he sees two men in a boat, one rowing and the other fishing. The fisher directs him to his house, near river and near wood, where he may spend the night.

He follows the fisher's directions and finally locates the castle in a valley. Crossing the drawbridge, he is met by four youths who disarm him and bring him fresh clothes. He is then led to a room adjoining the hall, from which come two youths sent by the host to escort him. They bring him into the hall, where he meets his host, a handsome, graying man dressed in black. The lord begs to be excused for not rising, since he is unable to do so, and invites Perceval to sit beside him on a couch before a fire, which is burning brightly.

While they are talking a youth enters the hall with a sword, sent by the host's niece, which he hands to the lord of the castle, who immediately girds it onto Perceval. "Fair lord," he says to Perceval, "this sword was judged and destined for you." Next there passes through the hall a strange procession, led by a youth carrying a white lance, from the point of which there issues a drop of blood which flows down the lance to the bearer's hand. There follow two youths with golden candelabra,

23

and behind these a fair damsel holding a grail *(graal)* in her
hands, followed by another damsel carrying a silver tray *(tail_
leor)*. At the appearance of the grail, a great brightness fills
the hall. Perceval watches this procession until it passes into
another chamber, but he says nothing to his host and does not
question him about the lance or the grail because he remembers the injunction of his tutor against too much talking. (Chrétien remarks here that it is just as possible to say too little
as it is to say too much.) The lord and his guest then sit down
to eat at a beautiful table. As each dish is served them, the
hero sees the grail simultaneously pass in front of him completely uncovered *(trestot descovert)*, but he fails to ask whom
they serve with it.

After dinner the host bids Perceval good night and is carried
by four sergeants to his chamber. Perceval is helped into bed
by the other youths who had remained in the hall. In the morning he awakens to find the castle apparently empty, so that he
has to dress and arm himself. As he goes past the chambers
which he had seen opened the night before, he finds them well
closed. He knocks and pushes, but there is no response. Going down the stairs, he finds that his horse has been saddled,
but when he rides through the castle he sees not a sign of life.
As he crosses the drawbridge his horse gives a great leap
and barely makes the other side, for the drawbridge has been
suddenly raised. The youth turns around and calls out, but
there is no answer.

Before beginning an analysis of this famous episode, it might
be well to acknowledge the fact that the grail castle is indeed
"holy ground" in more than one sense, and my interpretation
of its meaning is by no means designed to dispel the aura of
the marvelous which has surrounded it. In fact I shall try to
show that the meaning of the whole scene involves an authentic
mystery, human and divine, and that the mysterious quality of
the surface narrative, understood in its relation to the higher
meaning, is therefore a profound example of the harmonious
union of *sensus* and *sententia*, letter and spirit.

One preliminary matter that requires discussion here is the
nature of Chrétien's source or sources in relation to the grail
episode. Fortunately it is not necessary to deal with the problem at first hand. One of the most detailed and, in its main

conclusions, convincing studies of Chrétien's sources here is
to be found in R. S. Loomis, *Arthurian Tradition and Chrétien
de Troyes* (New York, 1949). Loomis holds that the grail theme
involves the intricate blending of two primary motifs: unspelling and vengeance (chapters lxviii and lxix). At the risk of
oversimplification, I shall summarize very briefly his conclusions. The unspelling quest, evident in the Welsh tradition
of Bran, became linked with a vengeance quest brought into
Wales from Ireland (the vengeance of Finn). Hence Bran, in
Welsh oral tradition, acquired features both of the wounded
kinsman who requires unspelling, and of the father whose
death the hero-son (Welsh Pryderi) is to avenge. With respect to Chrétien's source, therefore, Bran was ultimately
the model for both Perceval's father and the fisher king of the
grail castle. The question test in its relation to the grail (not
the lance) represents the unspelling; but the most pervasive
influence on Chrétien's narrative is the vengeance theme, which
provides the following motifs: (1) the Weeping Damsel (Perceval's cousin, whom we meet later); the Red Knight (slain by
Perceval at Arthur's court); and (3) the Dead Father (crippled
and later dying of grief). Following Loomis, we may epitomize
the vengeance plot approximately as follows: the Weeping Damsel rouses in the hero a desire to avenge his dead father,
struck down by the Red Knight. Loomis points out that Chrétien does not expressly associate the sword handed to Perceval
by his host, the fisher king, with the vengeance theme, but
that this connection *is* made in the continuations of Pseudo-
Wauchier and especially Manessier, where Perceval, after a
complex and baroque series of adventures, actually completes
his revenge.

  As a result of my own study of the *Perceval* from the point
of view of Chrétien's meaning, I am convinced that Loomis is
almost certainly right in assuming the presence of a vengeance
quest behind Chrétien's poem, and that this theme had an important influence on the poet even though he suppressed it as
inappropriate to his conception of Perceval's character. We
have already seen the undercurrent of a vengeance motif in the
Belrepeire episode, where Perceval's instinctive and genuine
mercy is contrasted with the implied ruthlessness of the potential vengeance of Gornemant de Goort and Blancheflor. It

is my opinion that touches of this kind reveal Chrétien's use (for his own purposes to be sure) of the very materials which he suppressed, if Loomis is correct, in their relation to Perceval. As regards the function of the sword, it is a part of my interpretation of the grail scene that the niece of the fisher king, she who sends the sword, *is* Perceval's cousin (whom he meets the next day as the weeping maiden), and I therefore offer the suggestion that in Chrétien's vengeance source her function was to present him with the sword. For Chrétien, of course, Perceval's cousin cannot serve to incite him to revenge; and this is perfectly clear from what she says when she points out to Perceval the road taken by the slayer of her beloved knight: " . . . but I have not told you because I wish, so help me God, that you go after him . . ." (3649-51). In relation to the problem of sources, however (apart from Chrétien's purpose), one cannot escape the feeling that the maiden is protesting too much; that, in Chrétien's source, revenge is precisely what she desired.

Most significant of all, I think, is the probability that the suppressed vengeance quest is the basis for Chrétien's elaboration of the role of Keu. Of course Chrétien may have known some form of the malicious seneschal motif, [12] and a similar role for Keu occurs in *Erec and Enide,* but then Keu's personality had already been suggested in *Kulhwch and Olwen,* and there is nothing in any of these accounts to explain Perceval's delayed promise to the prophetic maiden of the court to avenge the blow she received from Keu. Miss Adolf remarks that "it does not make much sense that Perceval, having won the Red Knight's armor and considering himself a knight, does not come back immediately to chastise the seneschal. "[13] My suggestion is, however, that Keu is used very skillfully, first, to expose Perceval's naïveté in the scene at court; second, to dramatize his achievement of knightly courtesy on his return to the court, by contrasting it with the churlishness of Keu; and, third, to provide a dramatic and climactic exhibition of Perceval's prowess (when he unhorses Keu and breaks his arm), while at the same time avoiding the necessity of a cruder and less original alternative, namely, a combat between Perceval and Gauvain himself. And I believe that this entire development was first suggested to Chrétien by the suppressed vengeance theme. That this belief is not entirely fanciful is, I think, supported by Loomis' contention that there was a tradition that Perceval was the *unwitting* killer of his father's slayer. [14] With this in mind note the fact that Perceval *unwittingly* strikes Keu from his horse (4466-77). What Chrétien has done here, with great economy, is to suppress the vengeance quest as inappropriate to his hero, only to let it reappear, diluted and harmless, in the highly functional motif of the "quarrel" between Perceval and Keu.

Turning now to the grail episode itself, we need first to consider what kind of episode Chrétien intended it to be. That it differs qualitatively from every other scene in Chrétien's poem is, I think, clearly evident in the text. When Perceval comes to the top of the hill, he first sees nothing except sky and earth (3035-49). Then abruptly he catches sight of the top of a tower down in a valley, where he finds the castle as directed. When he enters the hall and sits down beside his host, the latter asks him whence he has come, and Perceval replies that only this morning he came from Belrepeire. Whereupon the fisher king observes (3124-27): "'So help me God,' says the worthy man, 'too great a journey have you made today: you must have moved this morning before the watchman had sounded the horn for dawn.'"

To which Perceval responds, with characteristic naïveté (3128-29): "'Rather the first hour had already sounded,' says the youth, 'I assure you.'"

Chrétien's skill is evident in the two levels of meaning here: on the one hand, we have mere polite conversation; but, on the other, there is an unmistakable message in the fisher king's words: ". . . too great a journey have you made today. . . ." For it is surely true, as Nitze observes, that "the Grail castle was a sudden apparition," and that Perceval is now in a realm quite different from the real Arthurian world of the preceding episodes. [15] Lest the reader miss this vital point, Chrétien makes doubly sure by supplying a similar clue in Perceval's conversation with his cousin, the weeping maiden, after he leaves the grail castle. She points out to him that there is no hostel within twenty-five leagues where he might have taken shelter, so that she cannot understand (she marvels) why he looks so comfortable and rested (though as we shall see, in reality she does "understand").

Above all it is important to observe that no other scene in the entire poem receives this kind of careful preparation. We have already noted, it is true, that all previous adventures are related structurally to the internal development of the hero, and there are occasional overt suggestions of psychological depth (e.g., the staff of Gornemant de Goort and its possible suggestion of Perceval's crippled father), but in every case hitherto it has been clear that Chrétien is dealing with "real life" on the narrative level, whatever higher significance an episode may reveal in its development of the internal quest. But the episode of the grail castle, even on the narrative level, is a "sudden apparition, " and for a very good reason: it is the scene in which Chrétien presents his most penetrating analysis of the *débat* between prowess and charity taking place in the soul of the hero. It is also the crisis and the turning point of the entire poem.

The final point to be considered, before we come to a direct examination of the episode, is the identity of the fisher king. As we have observed above, in the discussion of sources, Loomis has concluded that the Welsh Bran was the model for both Perceval's father and the fisher king. Miss Adolf, though her study of the sources has an orientation somewhat different from Loomis', also observes that "the wounded king was thus originally the hero's father, not his uncle or cousin. "[16] To this I will only add that I believe Chrétien himself to have intended the reader to identify Perceval's father with the fisher king, and that, considering the nature of the grail episode as it has been defined (a sudden apparition), the fisher king *is* the hero's father. The details confirming this identification are very striking. Hence the safer assumption--barring the discovery of a document which shows that the poet merely turned his *livre* into verse--is that Chrétien himself arranged these details in the particular pattern that we find in the text. [17]

Let us now briefly consider the parallels that exist between Perceval's father and the fisher king in Chrétien's poem. In the first episode Perceval's mother, realizing that she cannot stop her son from going away, reveals to him for the first time that his father had been a worthy and famous knight. Then she goes on to tell him how he came to be crippled (435-41, 450-54):

"Your father, and you do not know it, was wounded in the legs so that he remained a cripple. His great lands, his great treasures, which he had as a worthy man, went entirely to ruin, and he fell into great poverty. . . . Your father had this manor here in this Waste Forest: he was not able to flee, but in great haste had himself brought in a litter, for elsewhere he did not know where he might hide. "

She goes on to tell Perceval that he was little more than two years old at that time, but that he had two brothers, who, encouraged by their father, left home to become knights. These two brothers were killed in armed conflict, and as a result the father soon died of grief. The fact that she must tell Perceval about all these events suggests that they happened before he was old enough to remember them.

With this let us next compare what Perceval's cousin tells him about the wounded fisher king, immediately following the grail episode (3507-33):

"Fair sir, a king he is, well do I dare say it to you; but he was wounded and maimed without fail in a battle so that since he has not been able to help himself, for he was wounded with a javelin through both his hips. He is still so in anguish because of it that he cannot mount a horse; but when he wishes to disport himself or undertake any amusement he has himself put in a boat and goes fishing with a hook; for this he is called the fisher king. Thus he takes his pleasure because he could not for anything suffer or endure other sport. He cannot hunt through the woods or fields, but he has his huntsmen who go to hunt in his forests, for this it pleases him to dwell in this retreat here, for in all the world there cannot be found a better refuge for his needs, and he has had built such a house as behooves a rich king. "

I have quoted this passage at length because every detail is important for an understanding of what Chrétien is doing here. First, note the parallels: both Perceval's father and the fisher king are wounded, the former "in the legs" *(parmi les janbes),* the latter "through both his hips" *(parmi les hanches);*[18] both live on as cripples. But the very differences that appear in these parallel passages have two highly important functions: first, to intensify what is already known to Perceval from his

mother's account; and, second, to materialize in a significant
way what was previously unknown to him.

An example from the first category is the fact that the host
is called a rich king, [19] which is an emotional intensification
of the mother's earlier statement (416-19): "'There was no
knight of such great worth, so dreaded nor so feared, fair son,
as your father was in all the Isles of the Sea.'" The second
category, materialization of what was previously unknown to
Perceval but open to legitimate speculation on his part, is illustrated by such genuinely pathetic details as these: the rich
king is still in anguish; hence he cannot ride a horse, he cannot go hunting through woods or fields, but fortunately--we
are consoled to learn--he gets a vicarious enjoyment from
the fact that his falconers, his archers, and his hunters can
hunt in the forest for him. Do we really need to be reminded
of Chrétien's description of Perceval in the opening lines of
the poem, riding his hunter through the forest and hurling his
javelins? Surely the poet could not have made the connection
more explicit than it is without dispelling the mysterious atmosphere that he has, with good reason, so carefully evoked
in the grail scene.

Thus the details in the description of the fisher confirm his
identification as Perceval's father, while at the same time they
exhibit a profound psychological verisimilitude. *The fisher
king's way of "life" is precisely what we could expect Perceval
to imagine as a setting for the memory of his father conjured
up by his mother's words.* That Perceval's cousin could in a
sense know what he knows, and that she is indeed a spokesman for what is in his mind, are issues that will be dealt with
in my analysis of the episode in which she appears.

Keeping in mind the fact that the grail castle is an apparition, and that the fisher king is the hero's dead father, we
are now in a position to consider the details of the grail episode as they occur. Perceval rides on his way from Belrepeire, praying continually that God will permit him to find his
mother alive and in good health. Chrétien tells us that this
prayer lasts until he comes to a swift and deep river, which
he dares not enter. He looks at the water and says (2990-93):
"'Ha! Powerful Lord God, if I could pass across this water,
I should find my mother beyond, as I think, if she is alive.'"

These lines are among the most dramatic in the entire poem. Ever since the hero has put off his Welsh clothes and renounced, so he thinks, the influence of his mother, the theme of remorse over his cruelty toward her has recurred with a crescendo of which these lines are the climax. And we will find that their reverberations extend beyond the grail scene itself to the point at which Perceval learns, with dramatic abruptness, that his mother is dead. Meanwhile, we need merely take note of his intense desire to see his mother. He does not yet know that she is dead, and we therefore will not expect to see her in the apparition which follows. But everything that Perceval does see in the grail castle, down to the very least detail, will be a direct projection of "what his mother told him."

Guided by the fisher's directions, Perceval comes to the castle where he is met by four youths who disarm him, take his horse, and dress him in a new scarlet mantle. They then lead him to the "lodges," apparently an area adjoining the great hall, from which point two youths, sent by the host, escort the hero into the hall and present him to the fisher king, who is seated on a couch before the fire, a handsome man, partly gray-haired, and dressed in black. "'Friend,'" he says to Perceval, "'may it not grieve you, if I do not rise to meet you; for I am not able to do so.'"

The stage is set for Perceval's experience. The son at last comes face to face with the father, the ultimate source of his desire to become a knight, and the scarred symbol of prowess, the ideal that has governed his life since the day he left his home in the forest of Wales. Standing with the son and his father, one on either side, as Chrétien describes it (3104), are the two youths whom the fisher king sent to escort the hero into the hall. And it is difficult to avoid the inference that these youths are Perceval's two brothers, the unfortunate young men whose premature death in combat sent their father to his grave.

To understand what happens next--the presentation of the sword--we need to realize that, whereas Arthur made Perceval a knight, and his tutor, Gornemant de Goort, put on his spurs, [20] it is the father who is to invest him with his sword. And why this sword, when he already has the one he took from the red knight? Surely it is because the hero must have the

sword which, like King Arthur's *Escalibor*, is to be exclusive-
ly identified with him, and which, indeed, is a symbol of his
own personality.[21] The sword is sent to the fisher king via
messenger from his niece, the golden maiden *(la sore pucele)*.
She is, as I have indicated, Perceval's cousin, the weeping
maiden. Her precise function will be dealt with below. Here
I will content myself with pointing out that she cannot actually
appear in the grail castle for the very good reason that she
is alive. Further, the fisher king's silent observation that this
sword will break in a moment of peril is designed by Chrétien
to prepare us for the maiden's later remarks; hence on this,
too, I shall defer comment for the present.

Rather, let us consider the message from the golden maiden
spoken aloud by the youth who brought the sword. He tells the
fisher king that the latter's niece sends him the weapon, and
that she will be glad if it is well employed. This is a significant
statement, relating to what Perceval's cousin says later about
the sword. He then adds (3154-57): "'He who forged the sword
made only three of them, and he will die[22] so that never more
will he be able to forge any sword after this one.'"

He who forged the sword is of course Perceval's father himself. He made only three, that is, he had only three sons.[23]
Two of them were killed. He himself has died ("will die" in
the apparitional tense); hence he cannot forge another sword,
or, in other words, cannot beget any more sons. And now,
with the austere reserve and objectivity of which only the dead
are capable, he invests Perceval, his living son, with the
sword. The hero draws the blade naked from the scabbard and
holds it in a grand manner, while behind him he sees the youths
(his two brothers?) standing around the fire which is burning
brightly.

The grail procession that follows the presentation of the
sword is so famous as to require no detailed review. And my
concern here will be primarily with the two objects that have
a symbolic function in the poem, namely, the bleeding lance
and the grail.[24]

The lance is to be identified with the hero's father, or the
fisher king, and the grail, containing the sacramental wafer
(oiste), with his mother, whose influence has helped determine
the form of the entire apparition which we are examining, but

who cannot be visibly present because Perceval does not know
that she is dead. In a deeper sense, however, the two objects
are the respective symbols of the components of Chrétien's
theme as I have defined it: prowess and charity. Why does the
lance bleed? Here is a mystery which, I venture to say, no
commentator, however learned, will be able to dispel. Why
indeed? It has bled, so to speak, ever since Cain slew Abel
in the field, and the reason for it is as old as the Fall. Here
is the bloody and ambiguous symbol of what has hitherto stood
as the motivating ideal in Perceval's life.

Opposite the lance, however, and in specific contrast to it,
is the grail, completely uncovered *(trestot descovert)*[25] before the hero, containing the Host, whose presence is perhaps
suggested to us by the other features of the procession--the
candelabra, the *tailleor* (= the paten?)--though it is not specifically identified in this scene because Perceval in fact does
not recognize it. And the Host, of course, symbolizes the
power of divine redemption, the one hope of deliverance from
the human dilemma, a fact that was doubtless even more obvious in the twelfth century than it is in the twentieth. Nevertheless, unfortunately for Perceval, he does not recognize it.
He does not speak; he does not ask the question: "Who is served
with the grail?"

It is an important feature of the meal that is served Perceval
and his host that simultaneously, at the serving of each dish,
the uncovered grail passes directly in front of Perceval. Here
it is necessary to recall what we have seen earlier about the
function of food in Chrétien's poem. When the young hero saw
the beautiful tent in the meadow, thinking it was the house of
God, he prayed for food and, fortunately for his physical hun-
ger, he found some inside the tent. Later, at Belrepeire, he
observed--no doubt with naïve disappointment, but presumably
with no enlightenment--that the two dilapidated abbeys were
lacking in food of any "value." Returning to the grail scene,
we see the two kinds of food, physical and spiritual, repeatedly
offered to the young knight, and along with this Chrétien builds
an atmosphere of mounting tension in one of the most remark-
able passages of the medieval poetic description (3213 ff.), so
that the charged silence of the hall seems to be shattered by
the unspoken imperative: *choose! choose!* But he does not

speak. He is on the verge of discovery, but he is not yet will-
ing to surrender to charity. He still clings to the ideal of prowess, or, as Chrétien puts it, he still remembers the advice of
his tutor against too much speaking. True, he tells himself
that he will ask about it in the morning; but, if he does not act
now, the insight that is hovering just out of reach will recede,
and tomorrow will be too late. The meaning of the unasked
question about the grail, which Chrétien finally discloses in
the Good Friday episode, will be dealt with later. Here I will
only observe that the answer to this question, if he had been
able to learn it, would have resolved the conflict in Perceval
between prowess and charity, which, as we have seen, is the
basis of the entire episode under consideration. But he does
not ask it.

Chrétien concludes (3310-11): "Thus he has respited the
thing and is intent on drinking and eating." The tension is
broken, and soon after dinner Perceval's host bids him good
night. Four attendants come in, and, grasping the corners of
the spread on which the fisher king is seated, they pick him
up and carry him "where they should" *(la ou il durent,* 3349).
Perceval, we may suppose, slept soundly until morning.

VII. THE WEEPING MAIDEN

(3422-3690)

Having departed from the grail castle, Perceval finds
some recent tracks of horses, which he follows in the
hope of finding those of the fisher king's household who
might tell him what he wants to know. He is following these
tracks when he comes upon a weeping maiden beneath an oak,
who is holding the body of a beheaded knight and lamenting and
praying for death. Perceval asks her who has killed the knight.
She replies that he was slain by another knight this very morning, but then, turning her attention to the hero himself, she
asks him where he spent the night. He tells her it was near
where they are, and she then asks him if it was the castle of
the fisher king. When he replies in the affirmative, she informs him in detail about the fisher, and proceeds to ask him
about the grail procession, showing that she is quite familiar
with the nature of his experience. When he admits that he failed
to ask a question about either the lance or the grail, she re-
proves him for it and asks him his name. He tells her it is
Perceval the Welsh *(li Galois)*. This is not only the first actual
occurrence of the hero's name in the poem, but also, apparently, his own first awareness of his name.

The maiden identifies herself as Perceval's cousin-german,
nourished with him at his mother's for a long time, and abruptly informs him that his mother is dead. She says that his sin
against his mother made him unable to ask the question about
the grail. Perceval suggests that she go away with him, and
pledges to overtake and fight the slayer of her *ami*. She re-

35

fuses, but shows him the road taken by the knight. Before Perceval leaves, however, she asks where he got the sword he
is now wearing and remarks that she knows who forged it and
that he should not trust it, since it will fly to pieces when he
goes into battle. When he asks how it can be repaired, she
tells him that no one can do it but Trebuchet the smith. Perceval then departs on the road taken by the slayer.

The conversation between Perceval and his cousin is very
important in its explication of the grail scene, and requires
careful consideration. We have already made use of it in iden-
tifying the fisher king, but it will now be necessary to take a
closer look, first, at the function of the maiden herself; second, at the position of the scene as a whole in the narrative
structure; and, third, at the hero's sword and what is said
about it.

Perceval's cousin is one of the most complex figures in the
entire poem. It is not a complexity of character, for she is
not treated "realistically" in the modern sense; rather it is a
complexity of function in relation to Perceval. Like every
other individual in the poem, she is important mainly because
of what she can reveal about the hero himself. First be it noted
that Perceval's cousin is "real" (as distinguished from "realistic") in the sense that she has real existence on the narrative
level and is not an apparition like the grail castle and its inhabitants. This is most apparent in the fact that she brings
him the news of his mother's death. Further, there is verisimilitude in the fact that she is Perceval's cousin. From
his mother's account of the destruction of their families (407-
88) we may infer the explanation for the presence of a niece
of one of the parents, orphaned by the conflict. More specifically, I suggest that Chrétien had the girl in mind at the beginning of the poem when he has Perceval tell the knight in the
forest that in addition to being called "fair son" and "fair lord"
he is also known as "fair brother." Of course "brother" can
be used as a general term, but the context here suggests family and household relationships (mother, sister, servants).
That the epithet does not refer to his two older brothers is,
as we have seen, evident from the fact that his mother has to
tell him about them. Undoubtedly it was his cousin, his foster-
sister, who called him "fair brother."[26] As she tells him, she

was nourished together with him at his mother's for a very long
time--thus the plausibility of her knowledge of the working of
his mind and his attitude toward his father, reflected in her remarks about the fisher king. So much for the reality of her
character.

A second function of the hero's cousin has to do with the narrative structure of the poem. She is a transitional figure, an
agent designed to bring Perceval back to reality. A similar
though inverse example of this is the fisher king. He is of
course an otherworldly figure, but he is first seen by the hero
as a fisher on the river, outside of the apparition, as it were,
in which he is to appear. Similarly Perceval's cousin, according to my interpretation, is the "golden maiden" who sends, via
messenger, the sword with which the fisher king invests the
hero--the sword being the one functional, material object that
Perceval brings with him out of the grail experience. It is in
this manner that Chrétien very skillfully and authentically
blurs the transition lines between the outer and inner worlds. [27]
The otherworldly being, the fisher, steps out to lead him in,
and his real cousin steps in as the golden maiden to lead him
out, that is, back to the real world of ordinary experience.

With the above considerations in mind, then, we can see
how Chrétien uses the maiden on the pyschological level as a
mirror of and a commentator on the state of Perceval's mind
when he emerges from the grail experience. They were raised
together as brother and sister. She knows him intimately. That
they do not immediately recognize each other merely shows us
one of those masterly uses of convention, having great psychological realism, for which Chrétien is so justly famous. There
is no need here for the masks or disguises used to build sus-
pense in conventional recognition scenes. At the time of their
meeting, both are preoccupied with their own experiences,
Perceval with the grail castle, and his cousin with the death
of her *ami*. The recognition unfolds dramatically in the course
of their conversation. Concerning the fact that Perceval's
cousin knows his attitude toward his father (the fisher king)
and sees the defect of his vision (failure to ask the question),
we may even infer, without violating Chrétien's text, that she
was a party to the conspiracy to prevent Perceval from ever
learning about knighthood and that she knew from his mother

the family history of which the hero was in ignorance until his
mother told him. Finally, as will be evident when we come to
consider her remarks on the sword, she shares his mother's
distrust of prowess as an ideal. In fact we may say that, in the
real world of the narrative, Perceval's cousin is the spokesman for his mother, now that the latter is dead.

Turning now to the episode itself of the encounter between
Perceval and his cousin, we find that it has, apart from the
sword motif, three main functions. First, it presents a re-
versal in what has been up till now (at least in the real world)
the steady advance of the hero. For the first time we see evil
resulting from his earlier actions. Though we do not learn
this until later, his crudeness in the Maiden of the Tent episode
has resulted in the death of his cousin's *ami*. No stress is laid
on this fact in the present episode, but it is of course an important feature of the Wretched Maiden incident which follows,
in which Perceval does his best to set things right.

A second accomplishment of this scene is to complete the
process of self-realization which we saw developing earlier
in Chrétien's symbolic use of Perceval's Welsh clothes. Similarly, in the present episode, at the precise moment that the
hero learns his name, he is informed of his mother's death,
which thus completes the severance of exterior maternal ties.
Surely this is the meaning of Chrétien's seemingly whimsical
account of Perceval's "divination" of his name (3573-77): "He,
who did not know his name, guesses and says that he had *Perceval the Welsh* for name, but he does not know if he speaks
true or not; but he spoke true, and did not know it."

One other general function of the scene under consideration
is to set the stage for the final revelation that comes to Perceval in the Good Friday episode. When his cousin learns that
he did not inquire concerning the grail and who is served with
it, she says (3583-92):

"Ha! wretched Perceval, how unfortunate you were then when you
did not ask all this, for you would have bettered so much the good
king who is maimed, for he would have wholly regained his limbs
and would hold his land and so great good would come of it, but now
know that great trouble will you and others have of it."

This passage is packed with meaning. The great good *(granz*

biens) that would have come refers both to the resolution of the
conflict within Perceval and the potential impact of this on society, as can be seen from its opposite, the great trouble
(grant enui) that the hero and others *(et autrui)* will have because of his failure. Chrétien reveals the social implications
of his failure in the Hideous Damsel episode; the resolution
of his personal conflict comes, of course, on Good Friday.
These will be taken up as they occur in the text. Suffice it to
say here that the reference to the healing of the maimed king
is Chrétien's hint that if Perceval could ask the question, and
know the answer, his father (that is, Perceval's mental image
of him) could "rest in peace."

The final problem to be considered in this episode is the
meaning of the sword. As we have noted, the sword stands for
Perceval himself. This is borne out by what his cousin says
about it. First she observes that it has never drawn blood from
man, and has never been drawn in need. This simply indicates
that the hero, though he has now reached maturity, has not yet
been scarred in the "battle" of this life and has not yet set his
face in the wrong direction. It is not too late for him to follow
the strait gate of charity, that is, to take "the sword of the
Spirit" (Eph. 6:17). As she indicated in her message to the
fisher king (3151-53), Perceval's cousin would be very glad if
this sword were well employed *(bien anploiiee)* where it is
given. On the other hand, however, she is quite aware of the
still powerful influence of prowess in his life. Perceval is,
after all, his father's son. And so, sounding very much like
the hero's late mother, she warns him about the sword (3658-
63): "'I know well where it was made, and I know who forged
it. See to it that you never trust it; for it will betray you without fail when you come to battle, for it will fly into pieces.'"
With this statement compare what his mother had said to him
earlier (428-31): "' . . . it is well known in many places that
misfortunes happen to the worthy men who maintain themselves in great honor and in prowess.'"

Perceval, of course, takes all his cousin's remarks quite
literally. But in the very simplicity of his reply he reveals
that her perception of his state of mind is accurate (3664-67):
"'Fair cousin, one of the nieces of my good host sent it to him
yestereve, *and he gave it to me and I hold myself well paid*

with it . . . '" [my italics]. He is, however, sufficiently concerned about her warning to ask whether the sword could be
remade if it ever did break. She replies (3673-85):

"Yes, but there would be great difficulty *(painne)*. If anyone knew
how to keep to the road to the lake which is above Cotoatre, there
he could have it rehammered and retempered and made whole. If
adventure lead you there, do not go except to Trebuchet the smith;
for he made and will remake it, or never more will it be made by
any man who may attempt it. Take care that no other put a hand to
it; for he would not know how to succeed."

I have quoted her reply in full because it contains a detailed
projection of the coming resolution of the entire poem (so far
as Perceval is concerned), which takes place in the Good Friday episode. The reference to a great difficulty *(painne)* sig-
nifies, of course, the hero's eventual contrition (6263, 6315 f.,
6333 ff.); and the remaking of the sword in the lake by Trebuchet the smith, a typical motif, is clearly designed to fore-
shadow the spiritual counsel of the hermit on Good Friday,
whereby Perceval is "remade."[28] But, for the moment at any
rate, all this is lost on Perceval. He can think of his sword
only as the instrument of prowess (3686-87): "'Certainly, it
would be very grievous to me,' says Perceval, 'if it broke.'"

VIII. THE WRETCHED MAIDEN
(3691-4161)

Perceval continues on his way until he comes upon a wretched maiden, who, though she might have been beautiful, is now clothed in rags and riding a lean and wretched palfrey. When the hero greets her, she answers by implying that he is responsible for her plight and warns him to leave before her knight, Li Orguelleus de la Lande, returns and finds him there. He is jealous, she explains, and has only recently slain a knight for stopping her. The victim is clearly the beheaded *ami* of Perceval's cousin.

While they are talking the proud knight appears, threatening to slay Perceval, but first says he will explain his conduct and the maiden's condition. As it turns out, she is the Maiden of the Tent (episode II), whom the young Perceval had kissed roughly and whose ring he had taken. Perceval identifies himself as the responsible party but affirms the maiden's innocence. The two knights then meet in combat, and the proud knight is forced to ask mercy. Perceval grants this on condition that he also have mercy on the maiden, and that they both report to Arthur, telling the king that he was vanquished by the Red Knight, and informing the damsel struck by Keu that she shall be avenged. Li Orguelleus agrees to all these terms, and he and the maiden report to Arthur in accordance with the instructions.

At this point Gauvain appears for the first time in the poem. He is impressed by Perceval's prowess in overcoming Li Orguelleus de la Lande, and the king tells him the story of Per-

41

ceval's appearance in court. Arthur then swears not to spend
two nights in one place until he finds the hero. The king's
household sets out from Carlion.

The evil results of Perceval's earlier actions are most
clearly displayed in this scene. The important thing to observe, however, is the effect of this discovery on the hero.
For the first time in the poem he is described as registering
shame (3786). In a general sense, therefore, we see him here
vanquishing the sin of pride. Chrétien gives his adversary the
name *Li Orguelleus de la Lande;* but he also reveals Perceval's
shame in a less obvious and more skillful way through the
wretched maiden herself, who says, in describing her misery
(3794-95): '"It behooves me to sweat with anguish when anyone stops me or looks at me.'"

This is precisely what Perceval has just experienced. Her
shame is his shame. Again we see one of Chrétien's characters mirroring the hero's condition. Perceval's recognition
of this comes in his blush; but consciously, at least, he still
does not recognize the maiden as the one he had offended. She
knows him better than he knows himself (3807-10): '"Ha! my
lord, ' says she, 'thanks! Be silent and flee from here, so let
me be in peace. *Sin makes you stop here . . .'"* [my italics].
Her point is that he tarries and converses with her not merely
out of duty or curiosity, but because secretly he does know
that he is responsible for her condition. When she says "flee, "
she is offering him an escape from what he should recognize.
That he refuses it is not merely a display of courage; he is
determined to vanquish his pride. It should be noted, however,
that this combat with pride is only a preliminary. The real test
will be administered by the Hideous Damsel. But the fact that
he has experienced shame here, and humbled himself, will
assist him in meeting the subsequent crisis.

The function of the scene at Arthur's court, where Li Orguelleus and the maiden report as directed, is to set the stage
for the climactic return of Perceval to receive the acclaim
of chivalric society, the delectable reward for prowess, the
secret desire of every honorable knight. In a more conventional romance, this would be the final scene. Not so in Chrétien's *Perceval.*

IX. RETURN TO THE COURT
(4162-4602)

Snow has covered the ground when Perceval arises early in the morning and comes by chance to a field near the encampment of Arthur. In this field a flock of geese has been attacked by a falcon, which wounded one of them in the neck, leaving three drops of blood on the snow. Perceval stops and gazes at this "image" *(sanblance)*, and it so reminds him of the beautiful face of his *amie* that he falls into a lover's trance. Meanwhile his presence has been reported to Arthur, who orders him escorted into camp. But Perceval does not wish to be disturbed in his musing. The first escort, Sagremor, is unhorsed for his trouble, and then the arrogant Keu is given a fall in which his arm is broken and his collarbone dislocated. Finally Gauvain approaches the hero and courteously invites him to come to the king. Perceval responds to this sympathetic approach, and Gauvain leads him into Arthur's presence, where he is acclaimed by all as a noble knight.

The blood on the snow has a fourfold function in Chrétien's poem. On the narrative level it implements the action that brings Perceval back to Arthur's court. The motif of the quarrel with Keu, as we have seen, has been prolonged so as to provide this climax, but the actual conflict is minimized by the fact that the musing Perceval is unaware of Keu's identity. In this way Chrétien avoids any disturbance of the delicate balance achieved in this scene. The dogged pursuit of a quarrel by the hero would have marred his welcome and, even

43

more important, would not have been in keeping with his character as it has been thus far defined.

Another function of this scene is to provide a tableau: the
hero at the height of his sophistication, "discovered" on stage
in a lover's meditation. The point is that Perceval has not
merely fought his way to the top; he is also *cortois,* as Gauvain
observes (4459). He now has everything required for purposes
of worldly reputation.

A third function of this scene involves the symbolism of the
snow itself. It is no accident that Perceval reaches the pinnacle
of worldly success in midwinter. Chrétien has not, of course,
fashioned a detailed and explicit chronology for his poem, to
be stressed at every turn, but we should recognize, I think,
that Chrétien's settings often serve, as do his characters, to
reflect aspects of the hero's internal development. If Perceval
rides through a desert (6239), it is because there is a desert
inside him. Similarly, in the present instance, the snow symbolizes the winter sleep of his soul, the trance induced by his
intense concentration on the ideals and rewards of "this earthly
world" (1669).

The most important feature of the blood on the snow episode,
however, is its ironical function. Surely Chrétien makes his
meaning perfectly clear when he describes Perceval looking
at the three drops of blood (4197-98): "he leaned upon his *lance*
and looked at that image" [my italics]. The poet is here telling
us in his characteristic way that, instead of being reminded of
the beautiful face of Blancheflor, the hero should have been
reminded of the blood that dropped from the white lance.[29]
Even though his meditation is twice interrupted by armed con-
flicts, the "image" fails to communicate. In spite of the new
sophistication, this is the Perceval of old. Some squires in
Arthur's camp were the first to see him out there in the snowy
field, motionless, leaning on his lance. They thought, says
Chrétien, that he was drowsing. And they were right.

The meeting of Gauvain and Perceval is the meeting of
equals. As we have seen, Chrétien has developed the quarrel
between Perceval and Keu partly in order to forestall any need
for a conflict between his hero and the model of Arthurian
prowess. And, since the two are equated at this point in the
poem, it is important to note that Chrétien treats Gauvain here

with the utmost respect. He is indeed the embodiment of *sens,* as Nitze points out.[30]

Thus Chrétien reveals his integrity. He is not content to use a straw man as the model for Perceval's aspirations. Gauvain's *sens,* or worldly wisdom, represents the highest possible development within the limits of prowess. This is stressed by the poet in every conceivable way, but especially in the conversations between Gauvain and Keu. If Keu's sarcasm is occasionally incisive, nevertheless in the end the seneschal's crudities serve primarily to highlight Gauvain's poise and good judgment. Perceval may well rejoice when they meet, for Gauvain symbolizes precisely what the young knight has been striving to attain. But it is the queen who sums up most explicitly the meaning of the whole episode when she greets Perceval with these words (4593-95): '"May you be welcome here as a proven knight of high and fair prowess!"'

X. THE HIDEOUS DAMSEL
(4603-4746)

Returning to Carlion, the king and his company of nobles hold great festivities in celebration of Perceval's arrival. But on the third day there appears a hideous damsel, riding on a mule. She greets the king and all the barons, but turns on Perceval and publicly denounces him for his failure to inquire about the bleeding lance or the grail. She mentions the good that would have resulted if he had asked, and the evil that must follow from his failure. She then turns to the king and announces various quests, which Gauvain, Girflez, and Kahedin volunteer to undertake. But Perceval vows never to cease until he has learned the truth about the grail and the lance.

It is generally agreed that the Hideous Damsel is a messenger from the other world, or perhaps more specifically the grail messenger.[31] Certainly she reminds us of the widespread motif of the supernatural being, beautiful in her own realm, but horribly ugly in this world. It has even been suggested that she is the grail maiden herself.[32] Whatever the truth of her origin, Chrétien uses her here for two specific purposes. She is, first of all, a projection of Perceval's conscience. Coming when she does, at the height of the hero's prestige, she is extremely repulsive to him. He would like to ignore her, but he cannot. Her denunciation is public. Of course it will be noted that Chrétien says nothing of the reaction of the court to this sudden condemnation of their hero. And we must not, after all, look for this kind of realism here. The

46

public denunciation is designed to show us that Perceval will
not suppress the voice of conscience. And this is in accord with
everything that Chrétien has led us to expect. Contrast this
scene with the subsequent one in which Gauvain is accused of
felony (4747 ff.), where Agrevain is the spokesman for the
reaction of the assembled onlookers. Here the narrative has
more realism, but much less psychological depth.

The other function of the Hideous Damsel, supplementing the
first, is to give us (and Perceval) more information about the
meaning of the unasked questions. She first speaks of the good
that would have resulted from the asking (4668-74): "'You had
great leisure for it; in evil time did you keep so silent; for, if
you had asked it, the rich king, who is much dismayed, would
have been wholly cured of his wound, and would hold his land in
peace, which he will never have more.'" As we have seen, the
potential healing of the maimed king refers to the fact that, if
Perceval had asked the question, his father would rest in peace.
The Hideous Damsel makes this even clearer than did Perceval's cousin when she says that the king would "hold his land in
peace." She goes on to say that this will never happen. That she
is overly pessimistic here will be evident in the Good Friday
episode. Yet, when we remember her function as Perceval's
conscience, this very pessimism has an impressive psychological validity.

The Hideous Damsel next goes on to describe what is going
to happen as a result of Perceval's failure (4675-83):

"Do you know what will happen [because of] the king who will not
hold land nor be cured of his wounds ? Ladies will lose their husbands for it, lands will be ravaged for it and maidens disconsolate,
who will remain orphans, and many knights will die for it; all these
evils will come about because of you."

For an understanding of Chrétien's theme this is perhaps
the most important single passage in the entire poem. It has
an intensely personal meaning for the hero, and yet at the
same time it dramatically extends the horizon of the poem.
In effect the Hideous Damsel says to Perceval: ladies will
lose their husbands, as your mother lost hers; lands will
be ravaged, as were your father's; maidens will be disconsolate and remain orphans, as is true of your cousin; and many
knights will die, as did your brothers. With an almost savage

cruelty she strikes Perceval blow after blow in these words.
But it must not be forgotten that what we are witnessing is in
Chrétien's poem the cruelty of the hero's own conscience.
There can scarcely be found anywhere, indeed, a more com-
plex and penetrating analysis of internal conflict.

But why is Perceval responsible for the woes of a battle-
weary world? This is the question that he is not yet able to
answer. The answer will come in the Good Friday episode.
But Chrétien has been carefully and skillfully building up to it.
Perceval, as the smiling maiden prophesied, is to be the best
knight in the world. That is, he has within himself the power
to do more than merely perpetuate the prowess of his father
and knighthood in general. But the release of this power and
its benign influence on the world is contingent on the resolution of his inner tension: the struggle between prowess and
charity. For, though he could remove mountains, if he have
not charity he is nothing. It is the hermit who will teach him
this, and who will make possible the triumph of charity in Perceval's soul.

Gauvain, Girflez, and Kahedin announce their intention to
seek various of the adventures proposed by the Hideous Damsel (who functions here, of course, as a mere tool of the narrative), but Perceval says (4728-40):

. . . that he will not lie in a hostel two nights in all his life, nor
will he hear news of strange passage without going there to pass,
nor of knight who is worth more than another knight or than two without going to combat him, until he knows of the grail whom they serve
with it, and until he has found the lance which bleeds, and until the
proven truth is told him why it bleeds, never will he leave it for
any pain.

Here we see virtually the last example of irony that Chrétien
allows himself in the portrayal of his hero. Perceval still believes that prowess conquers all and that, if he exercises it
with sufficient determination, it will eventually lead him to the
answer he is seeking. But Chrétien's irony is benevolent. It
includes recognition of the fact that Perceval has now at last
consciously set out on the road that will lead him, in spite of
himself, to the discovery that eluded him in the grail castle.

XI. THE QUEST OF GAUVAIN
(4747-6216)

As the nobles in Arthur's court are preparing to undertake their respective quests, a knight named Guinganbresil appears and accuses Gauvain of felony. Gauvain must appear forty days hence before the king of Escavalon, whose father he is said to have killed. On his way there Gauvain stops at Tintaguel, where he wins the prize in a tournament as the champion of a little maid, the youngest daughter of Tiebaut of Tintaguel. Continuing on his way, he finally reaches his destination and is directed to the town of Escavalon. When his identity becomes known, he is attacked by some citizens in a tower, but the crowd is dispersed by the king of Escavalon himself. Then by agreement the battle between Gauvain and Guinganbresil is delayed for a year, on condition that Gauvain will seek the lance that bleeds.

It will be well to observe at this point that, with the exception of the Good Friday episode which follows this Gauvain section, all the remainder of the poem is concerned with the adventures of Gauvain (6514-9234). The text comes to an abrupt halt with line 9234. Presumably Chrétien died without finishing his work. I shall not attempt to deal with the later adventures of Gauvain (6514-9234), since the incompleteness of the poem makes analysis of this section hazardous. The following brief observations on the first episode should make it clear, however, that Chrétien planned to use Gauvain for a definite purpose, and that this purpose was in harmony with his theme as I have defined it.

49

Gauvain, as we have already seen, is the embodiment of prowess in its highest form. He differs from Perceval in that the latter, though he has taken prowess as his ideal, is destined to go beyond it. But Gauvain, humanly speaking, cannot change. It is therefore appropriate that he be sent in quest of the bleeding lance, symbolic of the dubious ideal to which his life is committed. It may be that Chrétien planned to let Gauvain achieve a limited vision of the destructiveness of his ideal. But, from what the poet tells us about him, his only reaction to the discovery would be tears of attrition.

That Chrétien intended a contrast between Perceval and Gauvain is further evident in the fact that, whereas Perceval's father was the victim of combat, Gauvain himself is accused of having slain the father of the king of Escavalon. I hesitate to go beyond simply pointing this out, but one can reasonably suppose that Chrétien intended eventually to dramatize this contrast. We saw this kind of thing lightly suggested, earlier in the poem, through a comparison between the vengeful attitude attributed to Gornemant de Goort and the instinctive mercy of Perceval.

Looking briefly at the two incidents in the quest under consideration, I would say in general that they are designed to give Gauvain some standing in the narrative. Up to this point he has been merely a figure, a tool in the working out of Perceval's development. But, if he is to function in any important way on the narrative level, he must receive some of the same kind of attention that Chrétien has devoted to the real hero-- Perceval.

The interlude at Tintaguel, corresponding in a general way with the Belrepeire episode, is, I think, designed in the way I have suggested to establish Gauvain's "reality" in the narrative. The scene cannot serve exactly the same purpose as Belrepeire, for Gauvain is not being "educated" in that sense. Rather it serves to display Gauvain's sophistication. Thus the poet treats the adventure whimsically, and indeed this is one of the gayest and most attractive episodes in courtly romance. It has been claimed that this scene is a later interpolation, but I do not see how anyone can deny that Chrétien composed it.

The other scene, Gauvain at Escavalon, corresponds to Per-

ceval's visit in the grail castle. The very striking differences
between the two episodes can be accounted for by the differences between the two protagonists. Gauvain lacks the intro-
version and latent perceptiveness of Perceval. Hence Chrétien
suppresses (though not entirely) the otherworldly character of
Escavalon, which, as scholars have pointed out, was almost
certainly present in his source. What he does emphasize more
strongly than the supernatural is also more suitable for Gau-
vain--namely, the familiar epic warning, the stumbling of the
hero's horse (5680 ff.).

The most important feature of the Escavalon adventure is of
course the reintroduction of the bleeding lance motif. Here we
first learn that Gauvain is to go in quest of the lance. Significantly, the person who knows all about the lance and suggests
it as the object of a quest is a vavassor whom Chrétien describes as follows (6088-91): "In the place there was a vavassor, a native of the town, who counseled all the country, for
he was of very great *sense*" [my italics].

Nitze has shown that more than any other trait Chrétien
stresses Gauvain's "sense" *(sans)*. [33] It is therefore interesting
to note the use to which this sense or wisdom is put by the
vavassor in his advice to the king of Escavalon (6125-28): "'By
whatever one can and knows ought one to grieve what one hates:
to torture your enemy I do not know how to counsel you better.'" Clearly, this is the wisdom of prowess: Hate thine enemy. It would of course be inimical to Chrétien's purpose
to attribute this attitude directly to Gauvain. But the potential
evil beneath the surface of Gauvain's *corteisie* is grimly reflected in the wise counsels of the vavassor. And the poetic
method here is precisely the same as that used in the delineation of Perceval's character.

Concerning the lance itself the vavassor remarks (6168-71):
"' . . . and so is it written that there will be an hour when all
the kingdom of Logres which was formerly the land of ogres
will be destroyed by that lance.'" This statement has suggested
to scholars that we have here the influence of another lance
tradition, since what is said seems so different from the concept of the bleeding lance in the grail castle. This may be true
as regards the source. But I have no hesitation in saying that
for Chrétien this is the same (symbolic) lance as before. The

prophecy about it in this passage merely constitutes a significant application of the Hideous Damsel's warning of bloodshed (4678-82): "'Ladies will lose their husbands for it, lands will be ravaged for it, and maidens disconsolate, who will remain orphans, and many knights will die for it.'"

Hilka has pointed out that the reference to the ogres is reminiscent of Geoffrey of Monmouth's *Historia regum Britanniae*, I, 16, where Albion (= Logres, i.e., Britain) is described as having been inhabited by giants.[34] But what about the prophecy of the destruction of Logres? It seems to me beyond doubt that this alludes to the famous account, also in Geoffrey's *Historia* (XI, 1-2), of the downfall of Arthur's kingdom. That this catastrophe will be brought about *par cele lance* (6171) accords perfectly with Chrétien's theme. It is the fanatical devotion to prowess, symbolized in the bleeding lance, that will destroy Arthurian society.

It is possible that what I have observed about the function of Gauvain and the nature of his quest will provide a method for perceiving the significance of the later, incomplete Gauvain narrative. The exploration of this possibility cannot be undertaken here. But there is one problem in this connection which is worthy of brief consideration: Why did Chrétien insert the quest of Gauvain at all, when without it the structure of his poem is so completely admirable as it stands? One reason, as I have suggested, may have been to develop a contrast between Gauvain and Perceval. But there is another possibility also. Perceval is destined to find charity, the love of God, in the Good Friday episode. Any further display of his prowess, therefore, would be hollow and meaningless, except in an allegorical action of the type that, as we have observed, is totally foreign to Chrétien's poetic genius. And it is my suggestion that considerations of this kind led the poet to shift his focus to a protagonist for whom *avanture* was still possible and potentially meaningful. To do otherwise would have been to destroy the romance frame of the poem. Chrétien did not live to complete the quest of Gauvain. But I consider it at least a distinct possibility that, if he had, this quest would have presented an unmistakable challenge to the accepted ideals of Arthurian society, and hence to those of chivalry in twelfth-century France.

XII. GOOD FRIDAY

(6217-6513)

Perceval continues in search of adventure for five years without once remembering God or entering a minster to adore the cross. During this time he sends sixty knights (one per month) as prisoners to Arthur's court. At the end of this period he is making his way fully armed through a wilderness when he meets a company of knights and ladies, all barefoot and in rags. One of the knights asks him why he is wearing arms on Good Friday, when Christ was crucified. Perceval did not know what day it was, and he asks them where they have been. They inform him that they have just come from a nearby hermitage, where they have taken confession. They point out the path, which leads through a wooded grove. When Perceval reaches the hermitage, he confesses his sins to the hermit and tells him of his failure at the grail castle. The holy man explains the meaning of the grail and instructs him in the duties of the Christian life. Perceval remains at the hermitage for two whole days, eating only the scanty fare that the hermit shares with him.

For the reader who has observed Chrétien's theme unfolding with gathering strength throughout the poem, much of the Good Friday episode requires little detailed explication. Yet it will be well here to call attention to some of its main features, and especially to note the impressive way in which the poet effects the resolution of the conflict within Perceval.

The opening lines show the hero wandering in his wasteland, still doggedly demonstrating his prowess for the sake of the

53

distant acclaim of the Arthurian court. But the ideal has turned
completely to dust. And his encounter with the penitents on
Good Friday provides the shock necessary to make him realize
it. The old story of the atonement brings tears. He is now fully
prepared, ready to receive the vision. When the company
tells him that they have just come from the hermitage, he asks
them (6307-8): "'For God, lords, what did you there? What
did you ask, what did you seek?'" Their reply has a tone of
surprise in it, as if to say, Why ask as though you expect to
learn something strange? The merest fool should know that
we've been to confession. They then direct him to the hermitage.[35]

Perceval confesses to the hermit that he failed to ask about
the lance or the grail when he was at the grail castle, and that
since that time he has forgotten God. He tells the hermit his
name. The holy man then informs him that his failure was
caused by the sin of inflicting grief on his mother so that she
died from it. He adds that, had it not been for his mother's
prayer to God on his behalf, he would not have endured as he
has through perils of death and prison. He then explains the
meaning of the grail experience in the following words (6415-
31):

" . . . he whom they serve it with is my brother; my sister and his
was your mother, and of the rich Fisher I believe that he is son to
that king who has himself served with the grail. But do not believe
that he has pike nor lampreys nor salmon: with a single Host *(oiste)*[36]
which is carried to him in this grail, the holy man sustains and com-
forts his life. So holy a thing is the grail, and [he is] so spiritual[37]
that to his life nothing more is needed than the Host which comes in
the grail. Fifteen years[38] has he been thus so that he has not come
forth out of the room where you saw the grail enter."

This passage contains all the information necessary for
Perceval to resolve his conflict and complete his internal
quest. The key to the resolution is to be found in that seemingly enigmatic figure, the king who is served with the grail.
Do not believe, says the hermit, that this holy man *(sainz hom)*
has any kind of fish as his food. Rather he is sustained and
comforted by the Host, the sacramental bread, the Body of
Christ. So holy a thing is the grail (it contains the *oiste),*
and the holy man himself is so spiritual *(si esperitaus),* that he

requires no other food. And for fifteen years he has been thus
sustained.

The grail king, especially in his relation to the unasked
question, has baffled nearly every commentator on the poem.
Nitze, in his discussion of sources, states the problem most
succinctly:

> To dispel enchantment the question has an unsuitable form. "Whom
> does the grail serve?" "Why does the lance bleed?" refer to two
> distinct persons: the Grail King on the one hand, and on the other
> the Fisher King--who would have been cured had the question been
> asked (vv. 3586 and 4670). Since the Grail King is actually served
> by the grail (v. 6419), the effective bearing of the question thus re-
> lates to the Fisher King, and the natural conclusion is that the ques-
> tion--in Chrétien's source--was ritualistic. I hesitate to go fur-
> ther.[39]

The most significant observation I have encountered on the
character of the grail king in relation to Chrétien's source is
made by Loomis, who calls him a double of the fisher king.[40]
I am convinced that that is precisely what he is. Whether the
division of the fisher king into two characters occurred in
Chrétien's source or was the work of the poet himself does not
matter, as far as the present interpretation is concerned. The
important question is, how did Chrétien make use of the two
figures? The answer is not far to seek. For Chrétien, both figures represent Perceval's father. The grail king, the "holy
man, " is the spiritual *(esperitaus)*, the fisher king, the material, image; the one is soul, the other is body. The details of
the hermit's description bear this out. The soul is fed by the
Host, not by pike, lampreys, or salmon--that is, mortal food,
suggestively alluding by contrast to the body as symbolized by
the crippled fisher king. Furthermore, the hermit says that
the holy man, the grail king, has been thus sustained by the
Host for fifteen years. This is the length of time that has
elapsed since the death of Perceval's father.[41]

We are now in a position to understand the meaning of the
unasked question: Who is served with the grail? It has two
primary functions. One of these, as we saw earlier, is to call
the hero's attention to the spiritual ideal, charity or love of
God. This was dramatized at the grail castle in the simulta-
neous appearance, time after time, of spiritual and material

food. Perceval was being forced to choose between them, and
we know that he chose erroneously. He did not ask the question; he concentrated on drinking and eating.

But that is not all there is to it. This brings us to the second
function of the unasked question. If Perceval had asked it, he
would have learned, not only that the grail contained the Host,
but that this very sacrament was being served to his father,
who, far from living on as a cripple in the pathetic and pagan
setting conjured up in the mind of his son, was even now sustained by the bread which came down from heaven, of which it
is written: "If any man eat of this bread, he shall live forever"
(John 6:51). [42]

Thus the unspelling quest of the source has become for Chrétien the "unspelling" of the mind of the hero. Perceval's "sin"
in the grail episode was the abandonment of "what his mother
told him," that is, the spiritual ideal, the love of God. He
could see only with eyes of flesh, and hence the king, the "holy
man," was not visible to him. For this reason he failed to
make the discovery that would have banished the apparition of
the crippled king--namely, the discovery that his father had
obtained the grace of God, [43] had inherited eternal life. In the
words of the hermit Perceval now discovers this truth, and
his quest is at an end. The tensions of his ideological conflict
have been resolved, and, in a most impressive way, the antag-
onistic images of father and mother have merged and become
one in the all-embracing love of God.

A final point needs to be made about the symbolic role of
the hermit in the resolution of the hero's conflict. On one level,
of course, he is simply the typical spiritual counselor. Chrétien's use of him in this way is very skillful. His instructions
are purposely made as homely and commonplace as possible,
because part of the shock of the hero's (and the reader's) discovery is the obviousness, so to speak, of the answer to the
question. We have already seen this reflected in the surprise of
the penitents at Perceval's ignorance. The very prayer that the
hermit teaches him (6482-91), though described in exotic terms
as an allusion to the earlier motif of the sword (3138-43, 3654-
85), is undoubtedly the Pater Noster.

A more profound function of the hermit, however, is his
symbolic role in the resolution of the mother-father conflict.

One of the evidences of this is to be found in the genealogical relationships enumerated by the hermit. These relationships should not be ignored; rather their purpose needs to be correctly understood. In my introductory remarks at the beginning of this study, I pointed out the "recognition" aspect of the hermit's genealogy. The specific way in which this operates in the Good Friday episode is to banish the apparitional nature of Perceval's grail experience. This has always been a function of the spiritual counselor. The inner experience of the penitent must be objectified by the confessor and made concrete. The hermit therefore objectifies Perceval's experience in the terms of the "recognition" motif of medieval romance: the grail king is his uncle, and so forth. Thus the grail castle is given a local habitation and a name, and Perceval learns with subconscious relief that there are no apparitions, that the world is understandable and therefore acceptable. [44]

But the most important point about the hermit's genealogy is his statement that he himself is the hero's maternal uncle, for it will be noted that Perceval, though he doubtless absorbs everything that is said, responds specifically and enthusiastically to this piece of news (6436-38): "'Since my mother was your sister, indeed ought you to call me nephew, and I you uncle and love you better.'" To this the hermit replies, as we may suppose with gentle irony, "'True it is, fair nephew. . . .'" But he then gives Perceval his instruction, and we never hear the relationship referred to again. What then, beyond the functions already enumerated, is the symbolic meaning of the uncle-nephew relationship? Surely the point is the identification of the hermit with the hero's mother, as is brought out dramatically in Perceval's reaction quoted above. In this very human way Chrétien discloses Perceval's final acceptance of his mother's spiritual counsel.

There is, finally, one other important aspect of the hermit's role, and that is his identification with the hero's father. As we saw in our earlier consideration of the meaning of the sword, Chrétien suggests a link between Perceval's father and the hermit. [45] But that this link becomes explicit in the Good Friday episode is, I think, not open to doubt. It is true that, like all great poets, Chrétien demands the reader's complete attention. Yet he at no time abandons his responsibilities as a poet. To see the truth of this we have only to compare the hermit's description of the grail king (6426-28): "' . . . [he is] so spiritual, that to his life nothing more is needed than the host which comes in the grail, '" with the description of the hermit himself that was given by the penitents in answer to Perceval when he asked them whence they have come (6302-6): "'Lord, from here, from a good man, from a holy hermit, who lives in this forest, *nor does he live, he is such a holy man, except of the glory of heaven'*" [my italics]. Thus the identification is clear. But not only that: it is a spiritual identification, reflecting Perceval's final vision of his father in eternal glory.

Everything that the poet tells us about the hermit, therefore, leads to the conclusion that he symbolizes the resolution of the mother-father conflict which is so important an instrument in the articulation of Chrétien's theme. And there is an admirable validity in the symbolic presence of mother and father in that miserable hermitage in the forest, witnesses to the rebirth of their son on Easter morning. Chrétien's closing lines are very simple, almost casual. But they are strong enough to bear the weight of the entire poem (6509-13): "Thus Perceval recognized that God on Friday received death and was crucified; at Easter Perceval received communion very worthily. "

> Einsi Percevaus reconut
> Que Deus au vandredi reçut
> Mort et si fu crocefiiez;
> A la pasque comeniiez
> Fu Percevaus mout dignemant.

CONCLUSION

Having examined the *Perceval* in detail, we need now, by way of conclusion, to look briefly at a few general features of the structure, characterization, and theme of the poem. For it should be apparent, I think, that Chrétien, in spite of his attention to the finest details, is also in complete command of the poem as a whole.

The two components of Chrétien's theme, prowess and charity, determine the narrative structure of the poem. The stage is set for this in the opening picture we get of the hero in the forest of Wales, and in the remarks and counsels of his mother. From this point prowess is in the narrative ascendant, while charity descends--it does not decline--into Perceval's inner world. The first pinnacle in the narrative exaltation of prowess comes in Perceval's deliverance of the castle of Belrepeire, but in the very midst of this development Chrétien builds a crescendo of references to the mother, representing the irrepressible call to charity. This has its climax in the prayer for his mother uttered by Perceval at the moment he sees the fisher on the river. The ascending and descending ideals then clash in the grail episode. There the victory, for the time being, goes to prowess. A second build-up, of a more complicated kind, then leads to the next pinnacle of the action, the return to Arthur's court, where Perceval's prowess is acclaimed by all. But at precisely this high point of worldly success, with dramatic abruptness, the Hideous Damsel appears and accuses him of failure. After this the descent of the ideal of prowess is rapid (in structural terms, not in the chronology of the narrative), while the love of God emerges strongly in the Good Friday episode to provide the resolution. There is an admirable symmetry in the poem. The meeting of young Perceval and the knights in the opening scene corresponds to his encounter with the penitents in the Good Friday episode.[46] The poem begins in spring, moves through the winter of Perceval's worldly reputation, and ends in the spring, at Easter, with the rebirth of the hero.

We should be grateful if Chrétien had done nothing more than to achieve this structural perfection. But his delineation of the hero's character is at least equally impressive in its psychological complexity. That he is an innovator in this respect is, I think, established beyond the shadow of a doubt. But of course innovations of this kind are never completely new. The most striking feature of the internal quest in the *Perceval*, for example, is the use of the unspelling motif to provide a meeting between the hero and his dead father. For this basic idea Chrétien had to look no farther than the sixth book of Vergil's *Aeneid*, where is to be found the famous and justly admired account of Aeneas' visit with Anchises, his dead father, in Hades.[47] That Chrétien knew Vergil is hardly open to doubt, and that he was influenced in the *Perceval* by Book VI of the *Aeneid* can be considered entirely possible, so long as we understand that "influences" are not limited to verbal parallels, and that they can be sublimated and diffused throughout an entire composition. And, if we accurately assess Chrétien's poetic technique, we shall not expect him to use Vergil in the way that Dante does in the *Divina Commedia*.

The nature of the psychological complexity of Chrétien's poem can best be illustrated by his definition of Perceval's sin. The hermit tells him that his sin was the grief he caused his mother. But Chrétien makes it clear that the sin actually runs deeper than that. Her grief is not merely that of a mother's admirable but nevertheless sentimental attachment. It is grief over Perceval's rejection of what she has tried to teach him-- the love of God. Yet at the same time, as we have observed, there is a defect in her vision that gives Perceval's cruelty toward her a certain inevitability: she cannot bring her son into perfect charity while hiding him from the world. Hence his sin is presented to us with the most striking psychological realism. It is three-dimensional, so to speak, it is dynamic, and should not be confused with the more or less statically conceived sins of worldly knights in the later grail romances. Perceval's sin is a real sin, theologically speaking; yet Chrétien's mode of presenting it is not theological but poetic. He does not have to dress Perceval in a scarlet robe to make his point.

There has been a widespread belief, influenced no doubt by the character of the later romances, that Chrétien could do no more than reflect in his poetry the ideals (prowess, courtesy, sense, and so forth) of his age. A typical generalization of this kind can be seen in Erich Auerbach's otherwise excellent book, *Mimesis:* "Courtly culture was decidedly unfavorable to the development of a literary art which should apprehend reality in its full breadth and depth. "[48] I hope that what I have said about the revolutionary nature of Chrétien's theme will help to counteract this attitude. For if the poem contains the challenge to the secular order suggested in the preceding pages, there can be no basis for the allegation that Chrétien is a mere spokesman for the noble life.

One factor that may have led to the idea that Chrétien was no more than a mirror of his age is the modern conception of his relationship with his patrons. The alleged dictation of story and theme by Marie Champagne in the case of his *Lancelot* is notorious, but, as D. W. Robertson has constructively suggested, we may have misunderstood the meaning and motives of both Chrétien and his patroness. [49] Unfortunately, the popular understanding of Chrétien's reference to Marie in the prologue to *Lancelot* has had its effect on what is assumed about the poet's relation to Philip of Flanders, to whom the *Perceval* is dedicated (1-68). It is very common to read of the poet's flattery of Philip, and it is easy to go on from there and suppose that the poem's theme was designed to present a flattering representation of his patron's secular interests. Nothing, I think, could be farther from the truth.

Chrétien's praise of his patron in the prologue to the *Perceval* is gracious, not servile (7-20):

Chrétien makes a sowing of a romance that he begins, and sows it in so good a place that it cannot be without great worth, for he sows

it for the most worthy man in the empire of Rome, count Philip
[of Flanders], who is worth more than Alexander, who, they say,
was so good. I shall prove that the count is worth much more than
he, for Alexander had amassed in himself all the vices and all the
evils from which the count is free and pure.

He goes on to praise the count's ability to judge character, his
justice, loyalty, devotion to Holy Church, and his generosity,
which, says Chrétien, is free of any taint of hypocrisy or desire for worldly recognition and is motivated entirely by charity. He concludes (47-60):

God is charity; and he who dwelleth in charity, according to the
story (Saint Paul said it and I read it), dwelleth in God, and God in
him. Therefore know well of truth that the gifts which the good count
Philip gives are of charity, for never does anyone advise him of them
except his noble, debonair heart, which advises him to do good.
Is he not worth more than Alexander was, who did not care for charity or for any good? Yes, never doubt it in any way.

In the comparison of Philip with Alexander the Great, Alexander of course represents prowess, and the Christian Philip
represents charity. To suppose that when Chrétien ranks Philip
ahead of Alexander he is being hypocritical is to fail to understand the meaning of his poem. Whatever shortcomings with
respect to charity we may suppose Philip to have had, he would
inevitably stand far above the pagan warrior Alexander in
Chrétien's eyes.

To return to the poem itself, it is an important feature of my
interpretation of the *Perceval* that the poem's *sententia* or
higher meaning was clearly understood during and after Chrétien's own time. Admittedly the depth of understanding varied,
depending on the perceptiveness of individual readers, but this
is as true of a poem today as it was in the twelfth century. The
so-called "Christianization" of grail motifs in the continuations
of the *Perceval* and in the later prose versions is nothing more
nor less than the direct result of what was implicit in Chrétien's poem as it was understood by these authors. They did
not, of course, simply copy the earlier poet's ideas. The
author of the vulgate *Queste,* for example, pushes far beyond
Chrétien's human resolution of the conflict in Perceval to the
advocacy of a severe and ultimately dualistic Cistercian as-
ceticism. Prowess and charity give rise in this text to the

author's concept of earthly and celestial chivalry, whose spheres are so widely separated that no human hero can avail. That the author of the prose *Queste* understood and developed the theme of Chrétien's *Perceval* is true; but there exists no more decisive evidence of his self-defeating subordination of esthetic to doctrinal considerations than the fact that he saw fit to substitute an unearthly Galahad for Perceval as his grail hero. [50]

The later grail narratives in their relation to Chrétien's poem may be likened to the early Christian interpretations of Messianic prophecy. The latter exhibit an unevenness in the propriety of their citations of prophecies concerning the Messiah, ranging all the way from the inappropriateness of Hosea 11:1 (Matt. 2:15) to the crucial importance of Isaiah 53:7-8 (Acts 8:32-33). All of these prophecies, whether actually Messianic or not, testify to the intensity and power of their faith in Jesus as the Messiah. Simultaneously they reveal both a failure to understand certain prophecies and a profound comprehension of the basic point of the gospel: that Jesus was the Messiah. Similarly, the later grail authors, though they sometimes lose themselves in baroque detail and fantastic genealogies of Joseph of Arimathea, nevertheless reveal their grasp of the basic Christian message of the *Perceval.*

Finally, in the introduction to this study I asserted that the horizon of the *Perceval* extends far beyond the century of its birth. The truth of this assertion, if not already quite apparent, is, I think, confirmed by the fact that one of the most important poems of the twentieth century owes its ultimate inspiration to Chrétien's poem. T. S. Eliot, in *The Waste Land* (1922), saw the grail, of course, through the lens of Miss Weston, in a way that might have been strange to the twelfth-century poet. If indeed Chrétien thought of the maimed king as in any way symbolizing sterility, it would be simply the sterility of prowess as an ideal. He had no sense of the decay of civilization, or certainly no theory of history in the modern sense.

And yet Eliot's poem is in many ways reminiscent of his predecessor's. It presents the same challenge to the existing order, the secular ideal. Of course times have changed, and prowess has given way to science, though some scientists today would, I suppose, dispute the efficacy of the distinction.

However this may be, I think Eliot's picture of the twentieth-century wasteland is clearly revolutionary in its relation to the still potent ideal of science, or, as we call it, "the pursuit of knowledge" (to which should be added "for its own sake," more often implied than expressed). If Eliot in any way falls short of Chrétien's achievement, it is in the fact that his challenge is largely a negative one. The nameless protagonist of *The Waste Land* is Gauvain, not Perceval. His putative tears at the end of the poem are tears of attrition. And yet, given greater perspective, a later generation may discover a more positive theme. But for the present I must hold that Chrétien's *Perceval* stands as the greatest poem in the extensive literature of the holy grail.

NOTES

1. Perhaps the finest single study of *Perceval* is that of W. Kellermann, *Aufbaustil und Weltbild Chrestiens von Troyes im Percevalroman,* (Beihefte zur *Zeitschrift für romanische Philologie,* 88. [Halle: M. Niemeyer, 1936]). It is surprising to find that few *Perceval* scholars in recent years, especially in America, have taken into account or even alluded to Kellermann's work. Leo Spitzer wrote an appreciative review in *Modern Language Notes,* LV (1940), 222-26; and there are also the valuable judgments of Helmut A. Hatzfeld in his "Esthetic Criticism Applied to Medieval Romance Literature, " *Romance Philology,* I (1948), 305-27. My own acquaintance with Kellermann's book did not come about until I had largely formulated the interpretation of *Perceval* set forth in the following pages. Our methods of approaching the poem are different, in that mine is a more direct and specific effort to explicate the poem in detail; yet I have been encouraged to find much in Kellermann's analysis which confirms in a general way my own interpretation. And I must acknowledge a specific indebtedness to Kellermann for his observations on characterization in the poem.

A more recent scholarly undertaking is that of Urban T. Holmes, Jr., *A New Interpretation of Chrétien's "Conte del Graal"* (University of North Carolina Studies in the Romance Languages and Literatures [Chapel Hill, 1948]). This study has a closer resemblance to the present one, in that it attempts a direct and detailed explication of the meaning of the

text. Although I cannot accept Holmes's interpretation, I must
acknowledge the debt I owe him for calling my attention, through
his study, to the need for a re-examination of the poem.

Erich Köhler's *Ideal und Wirklichkeit in der höfischen Epik*
(Beihefte zur *Zeitschrift für romanische Philologie*, 97 [Tü-
bingen: M. Niemeyer, 1956]), arrived too late to influence
the formulation of my interpretation; it is, however, an excellent study in the tradition of Kellermann, whose ideas
are frequently accepted by the author. Köhler's approach to
Chrétien's romances (including *Perceval*) can best be described as that of the culture historian or, perhaps better,
the historian of ideas. He sees Chrétien's poems as the expression of a tension between the Ideal and the Real, with
the courtly heroine as the embodiment of the aspirations of
chivalric man. But the demand of the lady for sovereignty
(e.g., Guenevere in *Lancelot*) places an unbearable strain
on the union of Ideal and Reality which she symbolically represents, so that in *Perceval* the courtly heroine no longer
reflects the deepest aspirations of the chivalric hero, who
must now seek fulfillment in a purely spiritual realm. Köhler
then proceeds (in chapter vi) to draw a skillful analogy between the ideological developments of Biblical eschatology
and those developments which, in *Perceval,* imply a kind of
"chivalric eschatology." In this way, as the central figure of
a new chivalric soteriology (pp. 191 ff.), Perceval becomes
the "saved Saviour" of his society. This concept, however,
spells the end of chivalry and of the real world of the twelfth
century, and points toward the fullness of time (pp. 225 ff.).
I find much in this analysis to admire, and much that is in
perfect congruence with my interpretation of *Perceval.* The
bleeding lance is the guilt of humanity, the grail the salvation of Christ; the fisher king symbolizes the failure of chivalry (pp. 209 ff.). Where it seems to me that Köhler falls short
is in his detailed explications, especially where he attempts
to interpret with some precision what Chrétien intends to be
the meaning of the grail procession and the scene at the hermitage on Good Friday (pp. 212 ff.). His explanation is ham-
pered by an attempt to define Chrétien's accomplishments as
alterations of the "original" grail story in Robert de Boron's
Estoire; and, although his argument for the priority of Robert

is eloquent, it remains (to me, at least) an unconvincing one.
This approach particularly inhibits his discussion of the function of the old grail king (pp. 214·ff.), who is surely of central importance in his relation to the question *("cui l'an sert");*
yet Köhler is forced to assign him a subordinate role (p. 225).
In the final analysis, however, Köhler's book must rank with
Kellermann's as an outstanding study of the clashing ideologies
reflected in Arthurian romance, and of the paradoxical "guilt-
less guilt" of Perceval, the saved Saviour in a chivalric eschatology. Such a study inevitably adds a valuable dimension
to romance for the modern reader.

   Chrétien de Troyes: L'homme et l'œuvre, by Jean Frappier
(Connaissance des Lettres, 50 [Paris, 1957]), offers a popular
and yet scholarly account of Chrétien's poetry. Frappier gives
more space to *Perceval* (pp. 170-209) than to any other single poem. His most valuable contribution, in my opinion, is
his sensitive analysis of the process whereby in Chrétien *"Le
Saint Graal commence à remplacer le graal"* (pp. 204 ff.),
that is, the relationship of pagan source to Christian poem.
Here is an admirable illustration of the creative process that
medieval writers described as "clothing the naked falsehood."

   Other valuable studies of *Perceval* to which I am indebted
will be mentioned in the following pages. I trust that any in-
advertent omissions will be charitably regarded.

   2. R. S. Loomis, *Arthurian Tradition and Chrétien de
Troyes* (New York: Columbia University Press, 1949), p. 413.
The relation of Loomis' study of sources to the present interpretation is discussed below, especially in connection with
the grail castle episode (VI). One of the best brief studies of
Chrétien's sources, unpretentious but acute, is Helen Adolf,
"Studies in Chrétien's *'Conte del Graal,'"* *Modern Language
Quarterly,* VIII (1947), 3-19. Miss Adolf makes the identification of Trebuchet and the hermit referred to above in relation to Chrétien's sources (pp. 13 ff.). She sees the hero as
originally a son of the traditional clever artisan. Other features of her reconstruction of sources of the *Perceval* will
be referred to below.

   3. I wish to thank Robert W. Linker for permission to quote
from his excellent translation, *The Story of the Grail* (Chapel Hill, N.C.: The Book Exchange, 1952). I occasionally dif-

fer somewhat in my translation, but where this has a bearing on my interpretation of the poem I will call attention to the differences. For the text of the Old French original I use Alfons Hilka (ed.), *Der Percevalroman* (Halle: M. Niemeyer, 1932). I have also consulted William Roach (ed.), *Le roman de Perceval* (Textes Littéraires Français [Geneva: Librairie Droz, 1956]). A more recent English translation of the *Perceval* (omitting the Gawain adventures) appears in *Medieval Romances*, edited by Roger Sherman Loomis and Laura Hibbard Loomis (Modern Library ed.; New York: Random House, 1957), pp. 8-87.

4. Cf. Adler's comment in "Sovereignty as the Principle of Unity in Chrétien's *Erec*, " *Publications of the Modern Language Association of America*, LX (1945), 917-36, specifically p. 935, on the relationship of Enid and the damsel of the *joie de la cort* episode. They are identified as cousins.

5. E. Vinaver (ed.), *The Works of Sir Thomas Malory* (Oxford: Clarendon Press, 1954), pp. 268-73, 740-41.

6. For a general introduction, see his "Historical Criticism, " in *English Institute Essays*, 1950 (New York: Columbia University Press, 1951), pp. 3-31. More pertinent to the present discussion is "Some Medieval Literary Terminology, with Special Reference to Chrétien de Troyes, " *Studies in Philology*, XLVIII (1951), 669-92. A valuable earlier treatment of the subject is W. A. Nitze, "Sans et matière, " *Romania*, XLIV (1915), 14-36.

7. Robertson, "Some Medieval Literary Terminology, " p. 689.

8. This fact emerges clearly in the valuable study by Paul Pascal, "The Bible in the Conflict over Secular Studies during the Early Middle Ages, " *Classical Journal*, LI (December, 1955), 111-17, though Pascal is concerned mainly with the earlier period. He states (p. 111) that "a simple love of learning, including secular learning, that does not appear to be on the defensive, is not to be found before relatively modern times. " Cf. also J. W. H. Atkins, *English Literary Criticism: The Medieval Phase* (London: Methuen, 1952), especially chapter vi. Boccaccio's *Genealogia deorum gentilium*, lib. XIV-XV, shows that the defensive attitude was still strong in the

fourteenth century (cf. translation by Charles G. Osgood, *Boccaccio on Poetry* [New York: Liberal Arts Press, 1956]).

Since the completion of the present volume there has appeared a critique of the "historical criticism" advocated by D. W. Robertson, Jr. Cf. Morton W. Bloomfield, "Symbolism in Medieval Literature," *Modern Philology,* LVI (November, 1958), 73-81. Bloomfield states (p. 78): "It must be remembered that the advocates of secular literature in the Middle Ages were on the defensive. The pagan worldliness of much of it clashed with Christian otherworldliness, and those who loved the ancient poets were hard put to defend their poetry. The only way out, as the accessus and glosses to many a classical and pagan work show, was to argue strongly for the *utilitas* of such literature, and *utilitas* meant finding a moral meaning." This accords well with what I have called the "polemical cast" of much medieval literary criticism. Bloomfield goes on in his article to disparage the symbolic interpretation of medieval literature in a more general way, but his other points lack the cogency of the statement quoted above. The symbolic method cannot be refuted by frontal attack; its validity can be tested only through the study of individual literary texts.

9. Holmes's interpretation, referred to above (note 1), is in my opinion based on this kind of assumption.

10. Charles Muscatine, "The Emergence of Psychological Allegory in Old French Romance," *Publications of the Modern Language Association of America,* LXVIII (1953), 1160-82. The quotation is on p. 1168. His evidence is drawn primarily from the following romances: *Piramus et Tisbé, Narcisus, Eneas, Le Roman de Troie, Li Romanz d'Athis et Prophilias, Li Romanz de Floire et Blancheflor, Eracle, Cligès, Yder, Ipomedon, Florimont, Guillaume de Palerne, L'Escoufle,* and *Galeran de Bretagne.* See also Muscatine's recent book, *Chaucer and the French Tradition* (Berkeley: University of California Press, 1957), especially page 13, and the further references given on p. 252, n. 2. More specifically concerned with the psychological method in Chrétien's Perceval is Kellermann, mentioned above (note 1).

11. W. A. Nitze, *Perceval and the Holy Grail* (University of California Publications in Modern Philology, XXVIII, No. 5

[Berkeley: 1949]), pp. 281-332. The two quotations are taken from pp. 281 and 325.

12. Loomis, *Arthurian Tradition,* pp. 358-60.

13. Adolf, "Studies in Chrétien's *'Conte del Graal,'"* p. 15. She goes on to postulate two branches of the Great Fool story combined by Chrétien, one dealing with the Red Knight, the other with the Laughing Damsel.

14. Loomis, *Arthurian Tradition,* pp. 399-402.

15. Nitze, *Perceval and the Holy Grail,* p. 297.

16. Adolf, "Studies in Chrétien's *'Conte del Graal,'"* p. 10. See also her references to other studies, particularly those of Brugger and Newstead.

17. Loomis identifies the division or splitting of individuals as "fission." It is not clear to me whether he considers the fission of Bran to have occurred in Chrétien's source or to have been the work of the poet himself. In any case it matters not whether we conceive of Chrétien as responsible for the division or as merely utilizing for his own purposes a preexisting doublet in his source.

18. Variant readings cited by Hilka include, for line 436 *(les janbes), la hanche* BCHL, *les hanches* MQRU; and for line 3513 *(les hanches), les jambes* HLR.

19. That he is the *fisher* king may, of course, simply reflect Chrétien's source, as others have suggested, though, as will be seen later, the epithet *fisher* may include a specific Biblical reference (a variety of the phenomenon that Loomis calls "fusion").

20. He also girds on his sword, taken from the Red Knight along with the rest of his armor, but Chrétien does not call attention to this as he does to the spurs.

21. It is true, oddly, that in the *Perceval* (and nowhere else, as far as I know) Gauvain is the wielder of Escalibor. I have no explanation for this, unless it be that, in Chrétien's view of things, Arthur has surrendered his personality to Gauvain. It has frequently been observed by scholars that Chrétien commonly represents Arthur as weak and ineffective. This development would accord ideologically with the "feudalization" of Arthur in the French courtly tradition, whereby an original epic hero, whose leadership was maintained by the courage he

manifested in battle, gives way to a feudal king, an abstraction, a figurehead, to whom the real hero owes "allegiance."

22. The verb is *morra,* "will die, " as it has been usually understood and as it is rendered by Linker, *Story of the Grail,* p. 70. I see no need to translate "will desist, " as does Holmes in *A New Interpretation,* p. 9, no. 3.

23. Miss Adolf points this out in her study of the sources of *Perceval* ("Studies in Chrétien's *'Conte del Graal,* '" p. 13).

24. Once we understand Chrétien's poetic method, as I have tried to indicate in my introductory remarks above, we realize that there is no need to seek an exact correspondence for every detail of the description. To do this is to engage in dubious exegesis, not literary criticism. The candelabra and the tray *(tailleor)* are among the accidents, and not the substance, of the procession. Their function is limited to the scene in which they appear. The grail and lance, however, operate as important symbols throughout the remainder of the poem. It should also be said that in any effort to determine Chrétien's meaning, the physical appearance of the objects in the procession must be subordinated to their function in the structure of the poem. Thus, for example, the problem of whether the grail is a goblet, a plate, or a bowl must be subordinated to the fact that, as Chrétien later tells us, it contains the Host, the Body of Christ, the sacramental wafer.

25. There has been considerable controversy recently over the meaning of this phrase. Cf. *Romania,* LXXI (1950), 240-46, and subsequent volumes. Myrrha Lot-Borodine *(Romania,* LXXVII [1956], 254 and n. 1) supports Micha's view that "le Graal n'a *ni* voile, *ni* couvercle, qu'il est donc *trestot descovert. "* Without trying to explore the linguistic or archeological side of the problem (which I do not think can be finally determinative), I merely suggest that Chrétien here is trying to communicate the idea that the *Host (oiste)* was visible to Perceval *in the grail* if he wanted to or could see it--hence that the grail was completely uncovered.

26. Lines 343-60 occur only in MSS A and L. There is some evidence that Hilka considered passages of this kind spurious. Cf. Roach, *Le roman de Perceval,* p. ix, n. 5: "Hilka avait l'intention, qu'il ne mit pas à exécution, de publier dans la

'Romanische Bibliothek' une édition révisée de son texte de
1932. Elle devait présenter 'den gereinigten kritischen Text'
(cf. p. xxii de l'édition de 1932), ce qui veut probablement dire
que les passages qui ne figurent que dans les mss A et L en au-
raient été éliminés, comme ils le furent dans les morceaux
choisis de 1935; cf. les coupures après les vv. 342 (18 vers),
758 (2 vers), et 2200 (14 vers)." Whatever the significance of
the textual evidence, my opinion is that these lines (343-60),
which were known to Wolfram, are Chrétien's own. In this
instance, at least, the manuscript tradition represented by
AL suggests that copies of the *Perceval* may have circulated
while the poet was still engaged in revising it. Quite otherwise
is the case with the twenty lines following 3926 in MS T (Roach,
Le roman de Perceval, p. 115), where a later versifier has
supplied the breaking of the sword which he thinks Chrétien
forgot.

27. Compare the same phenomenon, expressed Hebraically,
in Amos 7:1-9, 8:1-3; Jeremiah 1:11-14, 24: 1-10.

28. Miss Adolf, in "Studies in Chrétien's *'Conte del Graal, '''*
pp. 13 ff. , states her belief that "in the original 'Grail' story
the hero was the son of a clever artisan," and that the name
"Trebuchet," a sobriquet denoting lameness, is suggestive of
other lame smiths like Weland, Daedalus, and Hephaestos.
Hence the lameness of Perceval's father, the fisher king, and
Trebuchet the smith. She concludes that "the scene at Trebuchet's was *replaced* [italics are the author's] by the scene
at the hermit's. "

I believe that Miss Adolf is correct in seeing features of
the mythical lame smith in Trebuchet, but was this a feature
of the original grail story? Loomis, in his reconstruction of
the vengeance theme, considers Chrétien's smith an intrusion
(Arthurian Tradition, p. 413). This theory accords well with
what I take to be Chrétien's purpose in the present passage.
Perceval is not yet able to understand matters of the spirit
and it would be useless, at this stage in his development, for
his cousin to direct him to a confessor. All she can do is refer
to the hermit obliquely, in the language of chivalry, as a smith
who can remake his sword if it should break. It seems to me
that her remarks about Trebuchet are simply Chrétien's ex-
tension of the sword symbolism and not an indication that the

smith was in the original grail story. The motif of the lame
smith was, after all, available to Chrétien in many popular
forms.

But if the "smith" is actually a symbolic reference to the
hermit in the Good Friday episode, then why is he called "Trebuchet," a sobriquet emphasizing his lameness? Miss Adolf
regards this as further evidence that the original hero was the
son of a clever artisan, and she cites two passages in support
of her conclusion. One is the messenger's reference to the
forging of the sword (3154-57); the other is the hermit's description of the prayer which he teaches Perceval (6481-87).
Now I would agree that these passages are related significantly
to what Perceval's cousin says about the smith (3673-85)--
but not because they are vestigial remains of an earlier version
sion of the grail story. Their relationship is rather an artistic one. Chrétien wishes to suggest an identification of the hermit with Perceval's father, for reasons which will be made
apparent in my analysis of the Good Friday episode (XII, below). A link between the two is provided here by the oblique
reference to the hermit as a lame smith. (Note a similar suggestion of paternal identity, mentioned earlier, in the staff on
which Gornemant de Goort was leaning when Perceval first saw
him [1352-59]).

Of course it is still possible that, in accordance with Miss
Adolf's theory, Chrétien found a surviving trace of the clever
artisan in his *livre* and simply used it for his own purposes,
as I have indicated. But before we conclude that details of this
kind are vestigial, I think it is always well to consider their
possible artistic significance. Not only is this procedure fair-
er to Chrétien, but it is also, I believe, in the best interests of
sound investigation of his sources.

29. Cf. C. B. Lewis, *Classical Mythology and Arthurian
Romance* (London: Oxford University Press, 1932), p. 265.
Although I cannot accept Lewis' identification of Perceval with
Orestes, it is interesting to note that he interprets the blood
on the snow as a call to vengeance (he quotes Aeschylus). The
general idea, of course, is as ancient as Gen. 4:10, "The
voice of thy brother's blood crieth unto me from the ground."
It may be, in view of what we have already seen above regard-
garding the importance of the vengeance theme in Chrétien's

source, that the blood on the snow originally had this function in the poet's *livre,* although I do not insist on this. The idea for turning the scene into a lover's meditation still seems to have come ultimately from the Irish Book of Leinster, as Nitze *(Perceval and the Holy Grail,* p. 311) and others have observed. It is possible that the fact that Blancheflor's hair is not black may account for the elimination of the raven in the source, though I believe it served primarily to stress the "image" of the red blood on the white lance. But surely the most important change is the introduction of the bird of prey, the falcon, which in this context is a pejorative symbol of prowess.

30. W. A. Nitze, "Gauvain in the Romances of Chrétien de Troyes," *Modern Philology,* L (1953), 219-25.

31. So Nitze, *Perceval and the Holy Grail,* pp. 320 ff.

32. Adolf, "Studies in Chrétien's *'Conte del Graal,'"* p. 14 and n. 75.

33. Nitze, "Gauvain in the Romances of Chrétien de Troyes," pp. 219-25.

34. Hilka, *Percevalroman,* pp. 733 ff., note to 6169 f.

35. Details of the description here are undoubtedly significant. The knotted branches (6325-27) probably suggest abatement of the flesh.

36. If there is any single word in Chrétien's text that can be called the most important in the poem, it is this word *oiste.* Throughout my discussion I have assumed that it is the sacramental wafer, and I fail to see how it can be considered anything else. To deny that the *oiste* is the consecrated bread of Communion is to deprive the poet of the very foundation and the climax of his poem.

37. The text (Hilka, *Percevalroman,* p. 286, v. 6426) reads: *Et il est si esperitaus.* Variant readings cited by Hilka suggest confusion on the part of some scribes as to whether *esperitaus* refers to *li sainz hon* (6422) or *li graaus* (6425). Linker *(Story of the Grail,* p. 143) translates 6425-28 as follows: "'So holy a thing is the grail, and so spiritual that to his life nothing more is needed than the host which comes in the grail.'" Thus he follows the variants in Hilka's footnotes. As far as I have been able to discover, Hilka's reading (cf. his note to 6426, p. 742) has been generally accepted. Cf. A. C. L. Brown, *Origin of the Grail Quest* (Cambridge, Mass.: Harvard University Press,

1943), p. 135; and *Publications of the Modern Language Association of America,* LXX (1955), 236, where the line has been rendered, respectively, "he is so spiritual," and "he is so much spirit." The reading of Roach's text *(Le roman de Perceval,* p. 189) also supports the view that *esperitaus* refers to *li sainz hon.*

38. The variant readings (Hilka, *Percevalroman,* p. 286) are: *.XI. anz* MQ, *Doze anz* BFHRTV, *.XX. anz* CPSU. My argument is not affected by these variants as long as it can be agreed--and the evidence seems conclusive--that the length of time intended by Chrétien falls somewhere within the general limits indicated by these variants, that is, from about twelve to twenty years.

39. Nitze, *Perceval and the Holy Grail,* p. 319. Holmes identifies the king as Christ *(A New Interpretation,* pp. 27 ff.), though he is led thereby to conclude that the *oiste* is not the Host and that the fifteen-year period mentioned by Chrétien is actually an indefinite number perhaps suggesting the elapsed time from the Ascension to the Arthurian era.

40. Loomis, *Arthurian Tradition,* chap. lxxv.

41. Perceval's mother tells him (458) that he was little more than two *(Po aviiez plus de deus anz)* when they came to the waste forest. At an unspecified time after this his father died, but presumably soon enough so that Perceval was too young to remember him. I suppose we could say that Perceval may have been as much as six years old when his father died. Thus fifteen years later, of course, Perceval would be twenty-one. As I have already indicated (note 38 above), the variant readings do not disturb this general picture.

42. For the identification of the *panis* of the Gospel of John, chapter 6, with the Host, cf. the *Glossa ordinaria,* Pat. Lat. CXIV, 383, on John 6:48 *(ego sum panis vitae): Ecce sacramentum verbis tegit.* The sixth chapter of John contains an extensive doctrinal elaboration of the feeding of the multitude with the loaves and fishes. Given the allegorical interpretation of the bread as the Host, it is easy to see how in exegetical tradition a contrast could develop between the bread and the fish. Note how emphatically the hermit declares that this king did *not* eat fish, but the *oiste.* Could this contrast have suggested to Chrétien the epithet *fisher* king for the *bodily* mani-

festation of Perceval's father? I do not insist on this interpretation, but it appears to be a distinct possibility. Of course
Chrétien's sources may have contained the epithet, so that
the presence of "fisher" in Chrétien could represent a fusion
of pagan and Biblical ideas.

The symbolic representation of Perceval's father in heaven
as a king who is sustained by the sacramental bread is very
striking, yet it does not in any way violate medieval theology
relating to the hereafter. To be sure, there is no Mass in
heaven, and Chrétien was undoubtedly familiar with the statement of St. John (Rev. 21:22), "And I saw no temple therein:
for the Lord God Almighty and the Lamb are the temple of it."
We need only remember that in the *Perceval* Chrétien is a poet,
not a theologian. A similar medieval poetic expression of the
joys of eternal life can be found in the Middle English dream-
vision poem, *Pearl*, ed. E. V. Gordon (Toronto: Oxford University Press, 1953). The maiden of the vision tells the dream-
er of the happiness which she and the other "kings and queens"
(448) are privileged to have in paradise. She says (861-62):

> þe Lombe vus glade3, oure care is kest;
> He myrþe3 vus at vch a mes.

> The Lamb gladdens us, our sorrow is banished;
> He brings us mirth at each Mass.

Clearly, since there is no Mass in heaven such as is celebrat-
ed by the Church Militant on earth, this statement in the *Pearl*
is symbolic (as is also confirmed in line 1115); likewise, in
the *Perceval,* the Host in the grail, with which the king in the
inner room is served, should be understood as the *symbolic*
representation of the salvation of Perceval's father, the "mirth"
which he receives "at each mass" in Paradise. As I have already observed, Perceval, at the time, was unable to "see"
this. The hermit explains it to him.

43. Cf. Hugh of St. Victor, *De Sacramentis,* II, viii.

44. Note that the recognition operates subconsciously. As
was pointed out in the introduction to this study, the hermit's
genealogy is not intended to be realistic, nor does Perceval
appear to regard it as such. The meaning of his comment on
his relation to the hermit is discussed below.

45. See note 28 above, and also Brown, *Origin of the Grail Legend,* p. 160.

46. I am indebted to my colleague, Daniel Weiss, for this and several other valuable suggestions.

47. In conceiving of Chrétien as a technical innovator in the grail episode, we must not overlook the skill and sophistication of Vergil's conception of Aeneas' experience, twelve centuries before Chrétien. Nor must we forget Vergil's debt to Homer, though it is true that the Latin poet nearly always makes his material over and assigns it new functions before using it. Observe Vergil's description of the dramatic moment when Aeneas, overcome with emotion, tries to embrace his father (vi. 700-2):

> Ter conatus ibi collo dare bracchia circum,
> ter frustra comprensa manus effugit imago
> par levibus ventis volucrique simillima somno.

Vergil uses the same description with reference to the apparition of Creusa (ii. 792-94). For a recent discussion of Chrétien's debt to Vergil (along with Ovid and others), see F. E. Guyer, *Romance in the Making* (New York: S. F. Vanni, 1954). Of course Guyer does not perceive any debt to Vergil in the *Perceval,* which he discusses pp. 221 ff. Readers of Middle English romances will recognize an excellent example (though the work of a lesser poet) of the conversion of a classical venture into Hades into a Celtic otherworld journey in the romance of *Sir Orfeo.* Another book dealing with Vergil's influence on Chrétien is Werner Ziltener's *Chrétien und die Aeneis: Eine Untersuchung des Einflusses von Vergil auf Chrétien von Troyes* (Graz/Cologne: Verlag Böhlau, 1957).

48. E. Auerbach, *Mimesis: The Representation of Reality in Western Literature,* trans. W. R. Trask (Princeton, N.J.: Princeton University Press, 1953), p. 142. Cf. also his delineation of Chrétien's romances as merely expressing *corteisie* through *avanture,* pp. 133 ff.

49. Robertson, "Some Medieval Literary Terminology," pp. 690 ff.

50. It is interesting to compare the high comedy of Chrétien's Maiden of the Tent episode with a similar scene, derived ultimately from Chrétien, in the prose *Queste,* where the al-

legorical method, on the analogy of scriptural exegesis, is quite evident. I quote from *The Works of Sir Thomas Malory,* p. 669. Percivale has been invited by an obviously allegorical damsel to lie down and rest on a bed in a pavilion:

And so he awoke and asked her if she had ony mete, and she seyde "yee, ye shall have inowghe." And anone there was leyde a table, and so muche meete was sette thereon that he had mervayle, for there was all maner of meetes that he cowde thynke on. Also he dranke there the strengyst wyne that ever he dranke, hym thought, and therewith he was chaffett a lityll more than he oughte to be.

With that he behylde that jantilwoman, and hym thought she was the fayryst creature that ever he saw. And than sir Percivale profird hir love and prayde hir that she wolde be hys. Than she refused hym in a maner whan he requyred her, for cause he sholde be the more ardente on hir. And ever he sesed nat to pray hir of love. And whan she saw hym well enchaffed, than she seyde,

"Sir Percivale, wyte you well I shall nat fulfylle youre wylle but if ye swere frome henseforthe ye shall be my trew servaunte, and to do nothynge but that I shall commaunde you. Woll ye ensure me thys as ye be a trew knyght?"

"Yee," seyde he, "fayre lady, by the feythe of my body!"

"Well," seyde she, "now shall ye do with me what ye wyll, and now, wyte you well, ye ar the knyght in the worlde that I have moste desyre to."

And than two squyres were commaunded to make a bedde in myddis of the pavelon, and anone she was unclothed and leyde therein. And than sir Percivale layde hym downe by her naked. And by adventure and grace he saw hys swerde ly on the erthe naked, where in the pomell was a red crosse and the sygne of the crucifixe ther in, and bethought hym of hys knyghthode and hys promyse made unto the good man tofornehande, and than he made a sygne in the forehed of hys. And therewith the pavylon turned up-so-downe and than hit chonged unto a smooke and a blak clowde. And than he drad sore and cryed alowde,

"Fayre swete Lorde Jesu Cryste, ne lette me nat be shamed, which was nyghe loste had nat Thy good grace bene!"

And than he loked unto her shippe and saw her entir therein, which seyde,

"Syr Percivale, ye have betrayde me."

And so she wente with the winde, rorynge and yellynge, that hit semed all the water brente after her.

BIBLIOGRAPHY

TEXTS

Hilka, Alfons (ed.). *Der Percevalroman*. Halle: M. Niemeyer, 1932.
Roach, William (ed.). *Le roman de Perceval*. (Textes Littéraires Français.) Geneva: Librairie Droz, 1956.

TRANSLATIONS

Linker, Robert W. (trans.). *The Story of the Grail*. Chapel Hill, N.C.: The Book Exchange, 1952.
Loomis, Roger S. (trans.), in *Medieval Romances,* edited by Roger Sherman Loomis and Laura Hibbard Loomis. (Modern Library, No. 133.) New York: Random House, 1957, pp. 8-87.

BACKGROUND AND CRITICISM

Adler, Alfred. "Sovereignty as the Principle of Unity in Chrétien's *Erec,*" *Publications of the Modern Language Association of America,* LX (1945), 917-36.
Adolf, Helen. "Studies in Chrétien's *'Conte del Graal,'''* *Modern Language Quarterly,* VIII (1947), 3-19.
Atkins, J. W. H. *English Literary Criticism: The Medieval Phase*. London: Methuen, 1952.
Auerbach, Erich. *Mimesis: The Representation of Reality in*

Western Literature. Translated by W. R. Trask. Princeton, N.J.: Princeton University Press, 1953.

Brown, A. C. L. *Origin of the Grail Quest.* Cambridge, Mass.: Harvard University Press, 1943.

Curtius, Ernst Robert. *European Literature and the Latin Middle Ages.* Translated by W. R. Trask.(Bollingen Series No. XXXVI.) New York: Pantheon Books, 1953.

Frappier, Jean. Chrétien de Troyes: *L'homme et l'œuvre.* (Connaissance des Lettres, 50.) Paris, 1957.

--------. "Du 'Graal trestot descovert' à la forme du Graal chez Chrétien de Troyes," *Romania,* LXXIII (1952), 82-92.

--------. "Du 'Graal trestot descovert' à l'origine de la légende," Romania, LXXIV (1953), 358-75.

Guyer, Foster Erwin. *Romance in the Making: Chrétien de Troyes and the Earliest French Romances.* New York: S. F. Vanni, 1954.

Hatzfeld, Helmut A. "Esthetic Criticism Applied to Medieval Romance Literature," *Romance Philology,* I (1948), 305-27.

Holmes, Urban T., Jr. *A New Interpretation of Chrétien's "Conte del Graal."* (University of North Carolina Studies in the Romance Languages and Literatures.) Chapel Hill, 1948.

Kellermann, W. *Aufbaustil und Weltbild Chrestiens von Troyes im Percevalroman.* (Beihefte zur *Zeitschrift für romanische Philologie,* 88.) Halle: M. Niemeyer, 1936.

Klenke, Sister M. Amelia. "Chrétien's Symbolism and Cathedral Art," *Publications of the Modern Language Association of America,* LXX (1955), 223-43.

Köhler, Erich. *Ideal und Wirklichkeit in der höfischen Epik.* (Beihefte zur *Zeitschrift für romanische Philologie,* 97.) Tübingen: Niemeyer, 1956.

Lewis, C. B. *Classical Mythology and Arthurian Romance.* London: Oxford University Press, 1932.

Loomis, Roger S. *Arthurian Tradition and Chrétien de Troyes.* New York: Columbia University Press, 1949.

Lot-Borodine, Myrrha. "Le *Conte del Graal* de Chrétien de Troyes et sa présentation symbolique," *Romania,* LXXVII (1956), 235-88.

Micha, Alexandre. "Encore le 'graal trestot descovert,'" *Romania,* LXXII (1951), 236-38. (See earlier article in *Romania,* LXXI [1950], 240-46.)

-------. "Deux études sur le Graal," *Romania*, LXXIII (1952), 462-79.

Muscatine, Charles. *Chaucer and the French Tradition: A Study in Style and Meaning.* Berkeley: University of California Press, 1957.

-------. "The Emergence of Psychological Allegory in Old French Romance," *Publications of the Modern Language Association of America*, LXVIII (1953), 1160-82.

Nitze, William A. "The Character of Gauvain in the Romances of Chrétien de Troyes," *Modern Philology*, L (1953), 219-25.

-------. *Perceval and the Holy Grail: An Essay on the Romance of Chrétien de Troyes.* (University of California Publications in Modern Philology, XXVIII, No. 5, pp. 281-332.) Berkeley, 1949.

-------. "Sans et matière," *Romania*, XLIV (1915), 14-36.

Nitze, William A., and Harry F. Williams. *Arthurian Names in the "Perceval" of Chrétien de Troyes: Analysis and Commentary.* (University of California Publications in Modern Philology, XXXVIII, No. 3, pp. 265-98.) Berkeley and Los Angeles, 1955.

Osgood, Charles G. (trans.). *Boccaccio on Poetry.* New York: Liberal Arts Press, 1956.

Pascal, Paul. "The Bible in the Conflict over Secular Studies during the Early Middle Ages," *Classical Journal*, LI (December, 1955), 111-17.

Pauphilet, Albert. "Au sujet du Graal," *Romania*, LXVI (1940), 289-321; 481-504.

Robertson, D. W., Jr. "Historical Criticism," *English Institute Essays, 1950.* New York: Columbia University Press, 1951, pp. 3-31.

-------. "Some Medieval Literary Terminology with Special Reference to Chrétien de Troyes," *Studies in Philology*, XLVIII (1951), 669-92.

Spitzer, Leo. Review of Kellermann (see above) in *Modern Language Notes*, LV (1940), 222-26.

Vinaver, E. (ed.). *The Works of Sir Thomas Malory.* Oxford: Clarendon Press, 1954.

Ziltener, Werner. *Chrétien und die Aeneis: Eine Untersuchung des Einflusses von Vergil auf Chrétien von Troyes.* Graz/ Cologne: Verlag Böhlau, 1957.